Side Effects

Hanna Prangner

Halo
PUBLISHING
INTERNATIONAL

Side Effects
Copyright © 2021 Hanna Prangner
All rights reserved.

ISBN: 978-1-63765-045-5
LCCN: 2021911216

Halo Publishing International, LLC
8000 W Interstate 10, Suite 600
San Antonio, Texas 78230
www.halopublishing.com

Printed and bound in the United States of America

To my husband and two daughters.
Los amores de mi vida.

Chapter 1

"I do," I muttered without any hesitation.

I looked down at my left hand and saw my husband place the gold wedding band on my finger. I stared into his eyes and couldn't believe this moment was actually happening. As I leaned in and closed my eyes, I felt the soft, gentle lips of my husband's kiss. He held my hand as we turned to his family and friends and walked down the aisle as Mr. and Mrs. Benk. I could feel everyone's eyes on us. I was now the wife of Jason Benk, the psychiatrist who fell in love with me, who married me. It was winter, December 15, 2023, in New York City.

"We did it!" I exclaimed as we entered the hallway leading up to our reception.

"Yes, we did," he said.

"How do you feel?" I asked.

Jason smiled at me and said, "I feel good."

I held his hand tightly; we could hear the guests being ushered into the hall. We stopped and stood together just as we heard Jason's friend say, "Everyone, let's welcome the bride and groom!"

We walked in together; everyone was standing, clapping, and smiling. I felt like a queen with her king. We walked over to a small table for two. We sat, and for a moment, it felt as if it were just us in that room. I sat staring at him, the lights dimmed, and I saw several waiters come out with the food. I was too excited to eat.

The night carried on, and just before everyone was ready to start dancing, Jason's dad stood up holding the microphone. He was a man of few words, but I knew that whenever he had something to say, Jason always listened.

"Good evening, everyone. I am Thomas Benk, Jason's dad. Jason, son, you have followed in my footsteps with your career. Now, as a young man—and at the start of your career, no less—you decide to get married. Well, to your new bride...welcome."

Everyone clapped. Jason's dad gave him a glare as he drank his wine.

Jason remained frozen, almost like a statue, until I said, "Hey, are you okay?"

He glanced over at me with glossy eyes and said, "I was just hoping he would say that he was proud of me." He looked down at his wine, and just as I picked up my glass to have a sip, Jason grabbed my hand and said, "You know you can't have alcohol with your medication."

I sat still, put my glass down, and said, "I was just going to have a sip, Jason."

"Laurie, please, as your—"

"You're not my doctor anymore," I whispered, quickly cutting him off before anyone else could hear what he was going to say. Even though we were sitting at our own table, I felt as if all eyes and ears were on us tonight.

Just then, the music started. Jason and I were being called for our first dance as husband and wife. He stood up, fixed his suit, and held out his hand. I grabbed it, and we walked to the dance floor. I looked into his eyes as I felt his hands wrap around my waist. I placed my hands on his shoulders and could feel his shoulders tense. He stiffened as we started to dance; I could tell his mood had changed. I wasn't sure if it was because of me.

Jason's parents came onto the dance floor next. He let go of me and began to dance with his mom, and I with his dad.

"Having a good time?" he asked.

"Yes, I am having a great time. Are you having a good time?" I asked.

"Yes. So, I assume you both are ready?" he asked.

"Ready?" I said, puzzled.

"Yes, Jason has work that needs to be taken care of in Colorado. They are expecting him in a month's time," he said.

I could feel my legs stiffen. I was hardly dancing as I said, "But Jason works here?"

"Not anymore," he said.

As we finished the dance, Jason's father smiled, and we walked over to Jason as he said, "Here is your bride."

I looked at Jason and said, "Can we go outside and talk for a second?"

I walked through the guests as they started making their way to the dance floor. The room was dark, with flashing lights, and the music was enough to keep everyone distracted from noticing that we were walking out.

I opened the door to the outside and felt the ice-cold wind; it was freezing. I stopped, turned to Jason, and said, "When were you gonna tell me about Colorado?"

He looked down and said, "Great, my father must've told you."

"Why didn't you tell me?" I asked.

"I was going to tell you," he said.

"So, it's true? You got a job there, and now we have to move in a month? What about your life here, your job, and our place together?"

"You really think I can stay here, Laurie?" he said.

"What is that supposed to mean?" I asked.

"Nothing…"

"So, now what?" I said.

"I figured you could go back to teaching," he said.

"Is that why Colorado? Because no one knows us there?" I asked.

"Do you want me to be honest?"

"Yes," I said.

"Then, yes…because no one knows us there," he said. He walked over to me, took off his suit jacket, and put it around my shoulders as he said, "It's a chance for us to start over, Laurie."

I exhaled and saw my breath in a cold fog. I didn't know what to say. I knew that I needed to try to enjoy this night; it would be my last winter in the city.

* * * * *

A few days passed, and what should have been marital bliss turned into a packing nightmare. I hated boxes, tapes, and Sharpies by this point. I never realized how much stuff we had until we had to put it all away.

"Wait, I thought we had a donation pile?" asked Jason.

"A donation pile?" I asked.

"Yeah, we can't take everything, Laurie. Remember? We signed a six-month lease on a much smaller apartment," he said.

"I forgot about the small part," I said.

"It's temporary, Laurie," he said.

I smiled and sat down on the floor of our modern, chic apartment. I was looking out the window and could see nothing but city lights lighting up the horizon. I could hear the hustle and bustle of the city, even though it was nighttime. The city never slept. It was my favorite thing about being here; the constant noise was relaxing to me.

"Hey, have you called Countryside Elementary School?" Jason asked as he brought me a glass of water.

I looked up at him from the floor and said, "No, not yet. I've been so busy with packing."

"You should call soon," he said.

I drank my water as Jason sat beside me on the floor.

"What are you thinking about?" he asked.

"I'm just nervous about this move," I said.

"Why?"

"I like it here."

"I like it here too, but I think that it'll help you more than you think," he said.

"Jason, if you're referring to what I think, then please stop."

"Laurie, I just think a change of scenery could be good."

"I know, Jason; you did always say it was all about the environment, right?"

"Right," he said.

* * * * *

The next morning, I woke up to a text from Jason: *Packing up the office. Call the school today.*

I sat up in bed, scrolled through my phone, and looked online at the school's website. I saw the name of the principal—Chelsea Halls. There was a picture of her. She had short blonde hair, green eyes, and looked as if she was in her midforties. I scrolled through the rest of the faculty. I saw the other second-grade teachers and felt a wave of nervous competition. If I applied there and got accepted to teach, then I would have to work with those other teachers who all looked much older than I was.

I dialed the number, heard it ring, and then, "Hello, thank you for calling Countryside Elementary School."

"Um, hi! My name is Laurie Benk. I wanted to inquire about the second-grade teacher position?"

"Oh, wonderful! I'll let the principal know; can you come in for a meeting?" she asked.

"Well, I'm in New York, but will be there at the end of the month," I said.

"Oh, okay. Well, I will notify Ms. Halls, and she will give you a call back."

"Great!" I said.

* * * * *

When Jason got home, he was holding Chinese food. I was starving. I sat down at the table, about to eat, when my phone went off.

"Hello, this is Chelsea Halls. I'm calling from Countryside Elementary School for Laurie Benk?"

"Hi, this is Laurie."

"Great! So you wanted to apply for the second-grade teaching position?"

"Yes," I said.

"Well, you would be working alongside our bilingual teacher; her name is Perla Guerrero. She will show you around the school. I just need your resume and to ask you a couple of questions if you have a few minutes?"

"Of course," I said anxiously.

"Okay, well, how long have you been teaching?"

"Oh, well, I worked here in New York at the Kiddins Private School as a second-grade teacher for about a year," I said.

"Wonderful, and what is bringing you to Colorado?" she asked.

"My husband's job. We just got married, and he's being, um, transferred," I said.

"Well, you will love it here, Mrs. Benk," she said.

"Great, I'm looking forward to a new—"

"Mrs. Benk? I'm sorry, as in Thomas Benk?" she said.

"Thomas Benk is my father-in-law," I said.

"Oh wow. Well, he is an amazing psychiatrist in the big city!" she exclaimed. "I read about his work, and I read about him in the paper, with how he helped that one woman."

"Yes, he is good at what he does," I said.

"I'm so sorry. I just realized that I recognized the name. Well, congratulations on getting married!"

"Thank you," I said.

"Well, I think this has been great, and I may be getting a little ahead of myself here, but I think I would really love it if you joined our staff. I just need a copy of your resume, proof of identification, and your social security card. When you come into town, if you can come by the school, we can get everything we need to get you started for August, seeing as how we have the semester left."

"Oh wow. I'm hired?!" I asked.

"Well, we really need a second-grade teacher. If everything else checks out, which I'm sure it will, then yes!" she said.

"Well, thank you! I appreciate it. I will send over my resume, and I have my references on there as well," I said.

"Great. Well, we will be in touch. Have a good evening," she said.

I hung up, and Jason looked at me as he ate an egg roll.

"Well, that seemed a lot easier than what I thought it would be," I said.

"What happened?" he asked.

"She hired me. I mean, I have to send my resume, but I'm hired!" I said.

"Oh, so what was the part where you said the father-in-law comment?" he asked.

"Yeah, she recognized the name."

"Oh, hmm, not Jason Benk?"

"No, not yet at least," I said as I walked over to him and gave him a kiss on the cheek. "Don't worry, people will know your name soon enough." I grabbed the Chinese food and chopsticks.

"That's the goal, right?" Jason said.

Chapter 2

Before I knew it, it was moving day. The moving truck came, and as I saw the movers load everything into the truck, I began to cry. It was a strange feeling seeing our life packed away in boxes. As the movers were hauling items, I sat in the center of the living room and looked around the empty apartment. I lay down on the wood floor and stared at the ceiling. I closed my eyes and started to remember the day I moved into this apartment.

* * * * *

Jason and I were on our second date when, after watching a late-night movie, he asked me if I wanted to come back to his place. I remember walking inside the building, being greeted by the doorman who said, "Good evening, Mr. Benk," and smiled at me as he stepped aside so that we could walk to the elevator to the top floor.

I gawked in awe as Jason opened the apartment's front door; the entire back wall was windows showcasing the beautiful view of the late-night city. Just as Jason was going to turn the lights on, I turned to him and said, "No, wait. Leave the lights off."

I could see his smile as he stood there watching me gaze at the city. He walked up from behind me, put his arms around my waist, and said, "Isn't it beautiful?"

"Yes. It's crazy how high up we are, don't you think?" I asked.

He laughed and said, "Is it anything like your place?"

I laughed and said, "Absolutely not."

"How much do you like the view?" he asked.

"I can't look away," I replied.

He leaned in and whispered in my ear, "Just stay."

"What about my stuff? I need to get my stuff." I laughed.

I thought he was joking until he said, "No, I can buy you whatever you need. I have furniture, I have food…"

As I turned around to face him, I said, "You're serious?"

He laughed and said, "Yes, why wouldn't I be?"

"We just had our second official date, and you want me to move in?" I said.

"Yes," he said with a grin.

"Well, I need my—"

He cut me off with a small kiss and said, "Laurie, you don't need anything. Just forget it all and stay."

* * * * *

I lay on the floor, with my eyes still closed, envisioning the memory. The silence was what stirred me to open my eyes.

Then, I heard Jason's voice echo in the now-empty room as he said, "Ready?"

"Can I have just another second?" I said.

"Laurie, we have a flight to catch. We should be getting our stuff in the next few days," he said as he stared down at his watch.

I got up and slowly began to walk towards the front door and him. He held the door open, and I turned once more to look at our home together. The door shut, and Jason locked it; he held the key in his hands, ready to turn it in.

We got in the elevator, and it felt so strange to be going down in it for the last time. I started envisioning what our new home would look like, so I turned to Jason and said, "What's the name of our apartment complex again?"

He laughed and said, "You always ask me; you forget so easily."

"I just realized that I only saw a few pictures of the place online," I said.

"Well, don't worry. You'll see it in a few hours," he said.

* * * * *

We got to the airport and checked our bags. I was so tired I didn't realize how badly I was going to miss the city. I knew Jason was aware that I wasn't happy about leaving, but I didn't want to keep getting sad and letting him see me so upset. We started walking towards our gate and stood while the previous passengers were getting off. I stared at them in envy, knowing they had just landed in New York.

Jason looked at me and asked, "Are you okay?"

"Yes...no," I said as tears slowly ran down my face.

"Laurie..." he said as he pulled me close and gave me a hug.

"I just love it here," I said.

"I love it here too, Laurie. I'm giving up a lot, you know," he said.

"I know you are," I said quietly. I knew what he was trying to tell me—he, not I, should be upset right now.

"Did you take your medicine this morning?" he asked as he still held me close.

I looked up at him and said, "Oh, I think I packed it."

"Really?" he said a little peeved.

"Now boarding, flight twenty-four, thirty-two in terminal thirty-two" was announced over the intercom.

I stood still and watched as Jason removed the flight tickets from the inside of his jacket and handed me mine. I took it, walked over, and handed it to the exhausted woman who looked as if she wanted to just sit down and drink a giant cup of coffee.

After she scanned our plane tickets, she handed them back and said, "Have a great flight."

We found our seats, and I asked Jason if I could have the one by the window. After sitting, I watched as everyone came on the plane and stowed away their things.

Jason sat down and exhaled. I knew he was tired too. I put my head on his shoulder and felt his phone buzz. He grabbed it, and I peeked at the text that got my attention: *Looking forward to our work. See you tomorrow morning.*

I looked at Jason and said, "You have to go to work tomorrow?"

He looked angrily at me, knowing I had read the text, and sternly said, "Yes, Laurie."

"But we haven't even moved in, and you're already gonna leave me alone in a new city?"

"Laurie, I'm not leaving you alone. I'm going to work, and, besides, you have to get to know the city sooner or later," he said.

I didn't want to get to know it so fast, right away, and alone.

I stared out the window as I felt the airplane slowly start to pick up speed. I never liked flying. I gripped Jason's hand, but he didn't bother to look at me; he just held my hand. I could feel the knots in my stomach getting tighter and tighter the higher we flew into the air. I heard the airplane bell as we reached 10,000 feet. I felt Jason let go of my hand, and I saw him wipe the sweat from his palm onto his pants. I was still staring out the window as I saw New York slowly fade away and hide behind the clouds.

I was calm by the time the stewardess came by to hand us our drinks. It was going to be a long flight, and I knew I needed to try to eat something before we landed. I had my plain water, and Jason had an old-fashioned.

"Are you tired?" I asked.

"I am. I wanna take a nap in a bit. Are you?" he said.

"I wish I could nap, but you know I don't like flying," I said.

He stood up and rummaged through the top cabin bin. I saw him pull down his work suitcase, where he kept his laptop, and heard as he was shifting things around. Then, I heard two clicks, and he zipped up his bag and put it away.

He sat down, leaned in to give me a kiss, and said, "I have something for you."

I laughed and said, "What?"

He looked at me and bit his lip as he said, "You are wound up, Laurie."

I knew he was right. I reached for his hand and felt two small round pills. "What is this?" I asked.

"Something to help you relax. I took one before I got on the plane," he said.

I grabbed the pills and quickly swallowed them. I wasn't good at taking pills. I always felt as if my throat was going to close up; sometimes I had to crush the bigger ones, but these seemed okay. I sat back and put my head on Jason's shoulder again. This time, I felt the heaviness in my body slip away as I began to slowly fall asleep.

Hours had passed when I woke up leaning against the side of the plane, close to the window. I had a blanket covering me now, and I saw Jason scrolling through his phone. I sat up and looked outside the window. I saw we were getting lower and lower, approaching the city.

"How long was I asleep?" I asked Jason.

"Oh, you're up. You were out," he said.

"Are we here already?" I asked.

"Yeah, we should be coming up to the gate soon," he said.

"I slept this entire time?" I asked.

"Yeah," Jason said.

I must've been so wiped out that it caught up to me, and I'd slept off my nerves on the plane.

* * * * *

We were exhausted by the time we finally pulled up to our apartment complex. Our new home was about a twenty-minute drive from the airport. I exhaled as Jason turned the key and opened the door to our new and smaller apartment. It wasn't modern; it felt like a cozy, cottage-themed apartment. I wasn't used to seeing so much brown and wood everywhere.

I looked at Jason as he said, "So, what do you think?"

I was walking around as I said, "It's okay."

I didn't get to choose it; the relocation was so fast, and the decision to rent this was done on a whim, just to get us here for work. I walked to the living room and sat on the floor. I looked up at the window and saw the view that we had was of trees. It was beautiful, but it wasn't New York.

Chapter 3

Our things finally arrived. It was nice to have a little bit of the familiar in our new place. Movers arrived to help unload, and the moment the first box was in the living room, I started unpacking. Jason was at work, so I was left to do all of this by myself, but these past few days, he was at his new office early and would come home in time for dinner. We had a trash bag, filled with Chinese food, that hung on the pantry door handle, and we slept on a blow-up air mattress. As the heavy furniture filled the empty apartment, I was already starting to wash dishes out of the boxes, throwing in a load of laundry, and hanging some clothes in our closet.

I sat on the couch and started taking out the framed pictures of us from our wedding. As I got up to place them on a nearby counter, Jason walked in holding another to-go order from our new, favorite, nearby Chinese food place.

"Chinese food again?" I asked with a laugh.

"It's good food, and it's close to home," he said.

"Well, I have been busy."

Jason glanced around and said, "I see that," as he handed me my sweet-and-sour chicken.

"I wanted to be productive. I'm just happy that our stuff finally came; it felt like it took forever to get here," I said.

"Yeah. Well, it's here now," he said as he sat down and ate.

"How was work?" I asked.

"It's good. I like it," he said.

"So, what are you working on that has you there forever and ever." I laughed.

"I wish I could talk about it, but I can't," he said.

I knew he had to be private about a lot of his work. But I was curious. "Do you have patients?" I asked.

"Yeah," he replied.

"Any...female patients?" I asked.

He laughed and said, "Laurie, please, let's not do this."

"I was just asking," I said.

Jason put his food on the coffee table, grabbed my food, also placing it on the coffee table, and leaned in to kiss me.

I couldn't help myself. "Jason, c'mon...do you?" I asked.

He sighed and said, "Yes, but I also have male patients. Everyone knows I'm married, and it's professional, okay?"

I felt weird for being jealous when he went to work. I know that he wasn't out looking, but when we met, neither of us was looking to be in a relationship either. I remember seeing him and being pushy, consistent, and very flirty. I also knew I wasn't going to be the only one who would vie for his attention.

"So, have you stopped by the school?" he asked.

"Not yet, but I sent out my resume…" I said.

"You seem nervous."

"Of course, I'm nervous. I mean, I know I wouldn't be starting until the fall, but that will come up before I know it, and I just don't wanna mess it up," I said.

"How would you do that?" he asked. I looked up at him, and as if he could read my mind, he said, "Laurie, that won't happen again. You're on meds now."

I sat on the couch and said, "Do you think I should tell them about my…diagnosis?"

"No, it's under control," he said.

He was right. I was fine now.

* * * * *

The next morning, I woke up early, called the school, and told them that I was on my way. I wore black pants and a white sweater. I swept my hair up in a bun and put a little lipstick on. I headed out and drove the short two miles to the school.

I pulled into the parking lot where I saw the sign that read, "Countryside Elementary School." As I walked towards the building, I saw some students outside playing. I smiled as I saw them running around. I walked inside and turned the corner, heading toward the office.

"Hi, you must be Laurie Benk." I was greeted by a familiar face; it was the principal, Chelsea Halls.

"Hi, it's so nice to meet you," I said.

"Please come into my office."

I walked inside a small room that looked similar to a psychiatrist's office. I sat down in the chair as she sat down at her desk.

She opened a file that had my name on it and said, "Well, thank you for your email. I got your resume, and I am just amazed at all of your credentials. I did receive the recommendation letter as well," she said.

"Thank you, I'm looking forward to starting here."

"Well, we are ready to have you for the fall. I will be teaming you up with Mrs. Perla Guerrero. She is wonderful and can show you around the school."

"That sounds great. Thank you so much," I said.

"I do have just one question," she said.

"Yes?"

"On your resume, you were at Kiddins and took a year off. May I ask why?"

Oh no. I didn't know what to say. I wasn't ready to talk about this and hadn't thought she would even notice.

"Oh. Well, during that time, I met my husband, and I was just so busy with planning our wedding," I said.

"Oh, I see. Well, wonderful, and congratulations again. I hope you like it here and you get settled in, and any questions you have, let me know." Before I left, she handed me a folder with everything I would need to know for the upcoming year. I also saw a note with the name "Perla Guerrero" and her phone number.

I walked back to my car and headed home. I was so excited to tell Jason that I officially got the job. I called Jason and got no answer. "Ugh, probably busy at work," I said to myself. As I drove, I sat and wished that I had someone to call, someone to talk to about this. But I had no one.

* * * * *

"Hello?" I said early on a Sunday morning. Jason was asleep, and I was surprised that I, not he, was the one getting a phone call at this hour.

"Hi, I'm so sorry. Did I wake you?" a woman's voice said.

"Oh…uh." I didn't know what to say.

"I'm Perla Guerrero. Ms. Halls gave me your number to contact you," she said.

"Oh, hi!"

"Hi. I just wanted to say welcome and to make sure that you knew, if you had any questions, to go ahead and give me a call."

"Well, thank you!" I said.

"Have a good day. Bye!" she said.

Jason turned to look at me and said, "She sounds nice, but she couldn't text you?" He turned over and lay on his back.

I lay down next to him and said, "Sorry."

"So, are you starting to like it here?" he asked.

"Slowly," I said.

I closed my eyes and fell asleep on Jason's chest. I could feel him breathing; his body was so warm. I felt safe in his arms.

* * * * *

The routine of waking up in the morning and not seeing Jason was difficult. I would turn over, and I could see the mold of his body in the bed. The sheet was flipped back, and I could smell the wafting scent of his cologne in the air. It was almost as if I were living with a ghost—I knew we lived together, but I only saw him when he came home.

I got out of bed and continued to unpack things. I felt as if I were always cleaning up here and there. Soon, I had enough used packing material for another trip to the dumpster. Walking outside to toss the trash was the only time I really stepped foot outside of our apartment. I strolled back inside and realized I had left the apartment unlocked; the door was slightly open, and I began to feel for a moment that I was not alone.

I shut the door quietly, not wanting to make any noise, tiptoed through the apartment, and heard a *thud*, as if something had fallen. It was coming from our bedroom. I thought maybe Jason was home early, but he would've made his presence known immediately.

I shouted out, "Hello, is anyone there?"

There was no answer.

I tensed up. Walking through the dark hallway that led to our bedroom, I heard the noise again. It sounded as if it was coming from our closet this time. I stood outside the closet door, exhaled as I held the doorknob, and pulled it quickly. I was expecting to see someone standing there, but there was nothing.

I closed the door and could feel my nerves fade. I began to feel light-headed. I grabbed my phone and called Jason. He didn't answer, and I threw my phone on the ground as I sat there, alone.

My phone started to ring. Jason was calling me back. "Hello?"

"Hey, you called?" he asked.

"Yeah, sorry. I thought someone broke into our apartment."

"What?" he asked.

"Yeah, I went to throw out the trash, and when I came back, the door was cracked open, and I heard a noise coming from our bedroom…but there was nothing here."

"Are you sure?" he asked.

"Yeah, I looked and—"

"No, are you sure you heard a noise?" he interrupted.

"Yes, loud and clear."

He sighed into the phone and said, "Laurie, did you take your meds today?"

"What does that have to do with anything, Jason?" I said angrily.

"You thought you heard something, and there's nothing. I think you're just freaking yourself out because you're home alone."

"Yes, I'm home alone, but—"

"Laurie, I'm working. Please try to relax, and take your meds," he said and then hung up.

"UGH!" I said out loud. I stood up and walked to the kitchen. I saw the small orange pills next to a bottle of water. I remembered taking them out the other day when I was unpacking, but I knew Jason had put them right on the counter with the water as his way of reminding me to take them. I took a pill and began chugging the bottle of water.

I was frustrated. I had so much left to do in the apartment, but I hated cleaning, doing laundry, and cooking. I was hungry, but I was more overwhelmed than anything. I walked over to the couch and grabbed a small blanket that was neatly folded with the other pile of laundry. I felt my head begin to feel fuzzy as I drifted off to sleep.

Some time passed. I heard the front door, started to wake up, and jumped up when I saw Jason was home. I could've sworn I was asleep for only five minutes, but it had been hours.

Jason stood at the door and said, "It's just me," as he shut and locked it. I sat up holding the blanket, and Jason said, "Feeling okay?"

"Yeah, I just got tired. It's hard unpacking all of this by myself," I said as I stood up and walked over to the kitchen.

"Laurie, I'm at—"

"Work, I know," I said.

"So, what's for dinner?" he asked.

I turned to face him and said, "Nothing. I thought you were bringing food."

"I've been bringing food. I just thought maybe you wanted to try something homemade, but it's fine. I'm not even that hungry," he said as he walked to the bedroom.

I felt horrible; I was still so tired and hungry. I drank my bottle of water, walked to our room, crawled into bed, and fell back asleep. I tossed and turned.

In the middle of the night, I heard Jason on his phone. He must've gotten a call from a patient. I tried to fall back asleep, until I heard Jason utter the words, "Thanks, Dad. I'm doing my part, and I think you'll be proud of me." I opened my eyes and lay there waiting for him to come back to bed.

After a few minutes, Jason turned off the hallway light, walked in, and sat on the bed. While pivoting to lie down, he jumped when he saw my eyes open and said, "Jesus, Laurie!"

I flinched and said, "What?"

He quickly turned the lamp on and said, "I thought you were asleep, but you're just staring at me…"

"Sorry, I heard you on the phone…talking to your dad."

"Oh, I was just talking about work."

"At three a.m.?" I asked.

"Let's go back to sleep. I have to be up in a few hours."

I leaned in to give him a kiss, but felt his cold cheek instead. He turned onto his side, with his back facing me, and I lay there in bed. I couldn't fall back asleep knowing he was upset about something.

Chapter 4

Three months had passed, and Jason was working more and more. He would get home later than dinner. I didn't know if it was because of the move, the not having friends, or the fact that a lot of the time I stayed in bed most of the day, but I started to feel less and less like myself. I was never really hungry, and I always stayed cooped up in the apartment. The blinds to the windows were always closed; I didn't like the feeling of people walking around and peeking inside our home, knowing that I was alone.

One day, I sat on the couch and decided to call Perla. "Hi! It's Laurie!"

"Hi, Laurie, how are you?" she asked.

"Good, I'm sorry it took so long for me to call you, but I was wondering if you wanted to meet and talk about everything for the fall?"

"Sure! How about Friday at eleven?"

"Great!" I said. I hung up with a little excitement, knowing that I was going to be getting out of the apartment for a while and maybe make a new friend. Even if it was just a work friend.

* * * * *

That night when Jason came home, I was so excited I said, "Guess what?"

"What?" he said as he held his work bag and walked inside.

"I'm gonna meet with Perla from work on Friday."

"It's about time," he said with a smile. He came over to me, sat down, and asked, "Laurie, are you doing all right?"

"Yeah, why?"

"I know you're alone a lot, and sometimes you don't make dinner. You wear the same pj's every day, and I don't see you eat. Are you depressed?" he asked.

"Depressed?" I said.

"Yes," he said.

"I just feel off…"

"Care to explain?" He leaned in closer to me as I sat down with my legs crossed.

I turned to him and said, "I haven't been wanting to say anything because I know what you'll say…"

"What?"

"Any time I tell you something is wrong, you ask me if I've taken my meds or to get out of the apartment for a while," I said.

"Laurie, I have seen you without your meds, and you aren't yourself at all. It's important to be consistent."

"Jason, this is why I don't talk about it."

"Okay, Laurie, just tell me what's going on," he said.

"I just feel sick sometimes...light-headed and tired, most days."

"Classic case of depression," he said.

I exhaled. I knew he could tell I was frustrated.

He stood up and said, "Look, I'm happy you made plans with Perla. Start to focus on work and making new friends."

He was right. I needed to start somewhere.

* * * * *

It was Friday, and I had set an alarm for 10:30 a.m. I was cutting it close to my meeting with Perla at 11:00 a.m., but it took so much for me to get out of bed lately. I walked to the bathroom and took a cold shower to help wake me up. I could feel the pins and needles of the numbing water.

I was freezing when I grabbed a towel and stepped out of the shower. As I was drying off, I was staring at the bed, wanting so badly to crawl inside of it for an ounce of warmth. I dried my hair, put on a little Chap Stick, some jeans, and a simple black tee, and headed out.

The place where Perla wanted to meet wasn't far. Everything was pretty close around here. It was a quaint coffee shop, and when I walked in, the heat of the room was immediately comforting. I closed my eyes for a moment, inhaling the aroma of the coffee beans. I walked over to the counter and ordered a hot black coffee.

I sat at a small round table and texted Perla: *Hey, I'm here. I'm wearing a white shirt.*

"Order up for Laurie!" I heard the barista call out.

I stood and got my coffee, sat back down, and saw this woman walk in—long, dark hair, glasses, flowing dress, and light-red lipstick. She was looking around the room.

She caught my gaze, walked over to me, and said with a laugh, "Laurie with the white shirt?"

I looked down and realized I was in a black shirt.

"Oh gosh, I'm sorry…my mind must've left me." I laughed and held out my hand as I introduced myself.

As we sat and laughed it off, she started the conversation and asked me, "So, what brings you here?"

"Well, I recently married, a few months ago, and my husband is a psychiatrist; he got a job here."

"Congratulations!" she said.

"Thank you!"

"Wow, marrying a doctor!" she said with a smile. "So, you are from New York, right?" she asked.

"Yes," I said.

"Oh wow, I'm surprised your husband got a job here."

"Why?" I asked.

"Oh, well, New York is such a big city, and here's much smaller."

I looked down and started to drink my coffee. I didn't know what to tell her. That she was right? That I hated that we moved? "It is a lot smaller," I said.

Perla began to talk about her life. She'd moved here because she got divorced, and then remarried shortly after. She'd also wanted a fresh start and ended up liking it; she said it had more of a small-town feel. Living so close to nature was what she had been searching for, it seemed; she said it brought her calmness.

I wish I felt the same. "Calmness? Being so close to the woods?" I asked.

"Yes, hearing the wind, and during the change of the season in fall, the leaves are just beautiful," she said.

I rolled my eyes without even realizing it.

"Well, maybe you just need to get used to it," she said.

Perla changed the subject from personal to work related. She started telling me what to expect at the school. I could feel my nerves start to tense. I knew she could tell. I had no idea why I was so nervous. I just knew that as much as I loved teaching, I didn't think I was ready to teach again after what happened.

"You can always call me if you have any questions. I'll email you the schedule as we get closer to the first day."

"Thank you, that would help," I said nervously.

"I think you will feel better when you meet the parents," she said.

"Meet the parents?" I asked.

"Yes. The parent-teacher meet-and-greet—parents come by and ask any questions and drop off their kids' supplies."

"Oh, that's right. I'm sorry. At the private school, it was just done a little bit different. I'm sure I'll get the hang of it," I said, trying to wrap up our meeting.

I got up and she smiled. Then suddenly, Perla frowned as she said, "Are you okay? You look a little pale?"

I wasn't fine. I wanted to crawl into bed; all I wanted to do was sleep. I didn't want to think about work.

"I'm fine, just tired," I said.

"Okay. Well, I will keep in touch; it was nice to meet you!" she said as she turned and walked out of the coffee shop.

I walked out, got in my car, and headed home.

I sat in the parking lot, staring at my apartment building. The car was off, and I started to cry. I had no idea what came over me. I don't know if it was the nerves of starting work in a few months or feeling nervous about having a friend here, but I couldn't stop. I looked up and saw people passing by. I didn't want anyone to stare at me crying in my car, so I put my sunglasses on, got out, and walked inside the apartment.

I didn't take off my sunglasses once I was inside; the darkness was comforting to me. I went to the counter and saw my pills there. I thought I took them before I left to see Perla, but I wasn't sure. I just needed to calm down.

I went to my bedroom and got in bed. I held my phone in my hand and saw a text message from Jason: *How was your meeting with Perla today?*

I didn't bother to respond right away. I lay in bed and fell asleep.

* * * * *

When I awoke, I saw Jason sitting on the bed. He was on his phone.

When Jason saw that I was awake, he said, "Morning, Laurie, sunny inside?"

I realized I'd slept with my sunglasses on. He must be thinking I look so crazy right now. I took the glasses off.

He asked, "Did you drink when you met with Perla today?"

"No," I said.

"Really? Please explain this."

He showed me a series of text messages that I had sent:

Where are you?

Come home now!

I think something is wrong with me. I am possessed or something, Benk.

I was shocked. I didn't remember sending anything to Jason, but when I grabbed my phone, all of the messages were there.

"I-I d-didn't s-send th-that. I-I know I-I d-didn't," I stammered.

"Laurie, it's on your phone, and I got them, which is why I rushed home, and I see you passed out in bed with your shoes and sunglasses on."

"Jason, look, I know I never sent anything like that."

"Laurie, you are always tired lately."

"I know!" I shouted.

"What is it then, Laurie? I can't be at home and at work," he said.

I looked down and said, "I know, Jason, I know…"

"I know you are going through stuff, but I need to know that you're stable while I'm at work," he said.

I didn't like that word—*stable*. It was a word he'd used often when I was his patient.

"Okay, look…whatever is going on, I'll deal with it. I'll be fine," I said.

"Okay, I trust you," he said.

I now knew that I couldn't tell Jason what was really going on—that I hadn't been myself, that most days I felt physically ill, and that I was always sleeping and barely eating. I had to lie and tell him that I was okay.

Chapter 5

July 21, it was the day of the parent-teacher meet-and-greet.

Perla and I had texted here and there throughout the summer. I felt as if I was getting worse, and I didn't want anyone to notice. Jason was so busy at work, but we also had to find a home, and quickly. We wanted to find a turnkey home before the end of August. It seemed almost impossible.

I was standing in the closet, trying to find a good outfit to wear. Jason was home, and he walked into the closet with me, stared down at the pile of clothes I kept changing out of, and said, "You'll be fine in whatever you wear."

"I want to make the right impression," I said.

I had a floral dress on, but I changed. I looked through my closet again, found my collection of pencil skirts, and decided to go with one of those, heels, and a dark-blue blouse. I walked to the bathroom, put my hair in a pony-tail, and applied a little lipstick and blush. When I started to put on my mascara, I saw Jason was now standing in the doorway of the bathroom, staring at me.

"What?" I said as I looked through my makeup case.

"Nothing, it's just been a while since you've looked like you," he said.

"I know; you've been seeing me in my pj's a lot lately," I said.

"Well, you're starting to get some color in your face," he said.

"It's the blush," I said.

"Well, whatever it is, it's nice to see the old you coming back."

I smiled and said, "So, any luck with the house hunting?"

"Yeah, there is one off of Mills Road. I have an appointment to see it."

I nodded as I finished getting ready and said, "Well, sorry I can't go to see this house with you, but you have good taste. I trust you."

"It's okay. There really aren't a lot of properties that have caught my eye, so we need to decide soon, Laurie."

I walked by him, grabbed my bag, and said, "Jason, do whatever you need to do."

He looked at me and said, "I got it covered, thanks for trusting me."

I kissed him goodbye and rushed out of the apartment to head to the school.

* * * * *

Once I got to the school, the only faces I knew were those of the principal and Perla. The principal waved at me

41

while she stood talking to a parent. I waved back and walked over to Perla.

"Are you ready for tonight?" she asked excitedly.

"Not really," I said.

"Don't worry, you'll be fine," she said.

We walked inside to her classroom. I saw a stack of papers for parents; it included a "What to Expect" sheet for the students, the bell schedule, and an introductory sheet about me with my picture. I picked it up and was surprised to see it there. I looked at Perla and said, "This is nice; did you do this?"

She nodded and said, "I want the parents to know that this year we are doing things differently with the classrooms. It is something new, and it gives them a way to get to know you and something to show their kids!"

She was right. I stood there rereading my introduction page, staring back at my photo on the page. Just then, I thought, *Where did she find this picture of me?*

"Perla? I don't remember giving you my picture?" I said.

She turned to me and said, "Oh, I Googled you."

I was a little shocked.

"I'm sorry. When you said you were from New York... and your husband being a psychiatrist... Chelsea had mentioned something about his father being well known... Are you upset?"

"No...no..." I said.

"I should have asked. I just needed something quick," she said.

"It's fine; it's just, um…"

"What?" she asked.

"Was there anything else about me?" I asked.

She looked confused for a second and said, "No, just this photo from a charity event."

I forced a laugh and said, "Oh, okay."

I put the paper down, and I looked down at the stack with my face printed on thirty sheets, hoping no one would recognize me.

I looked at the clock, and just then there was a knock on the classroom door. Parents began to arrive. I started introducing myself, and they smiled, took the papers on Perla's desk, and walked over to Perla. It didn't seem as if anyone really wanted to meet me.

I walked over next to Perla, and she spoke in Spanish to a few of the parents. I didn't understand what she was saying, but she looked so happy while speaking to them.

They turned to me, and one said, "*Hola!*"

I smiled and said, "I'm sorry; I don't speak Spanish."

They smiled, and one said, "Oh, I thought you were another bilingual teacher."

"Oh, I am the new teacher. I will be starting this year."

"Wonderful, have you ever taught before?"

"Yes, I used to teach at a private school in New York," I said.

"That's great!"

I laughed. At this point, I wasn't exactly sure what I was doing, or if I was even excited to do this anymore. I stood there in the classroom, completely motionless. I gazed as parents walked in and out. I stared as they walked in with bags of supplies.

I saw how Perla started sorting things and answering everyone's questions. She walked around with such grace. She was quick on her feet, wearing flats and pants, while I felt overdressed in my heels. Perla tried her best to introduce me; the most I would get was a few handshakes and several welcomes, but no one really wanted to talk.

I started to help Perla sort the supplies. As the sun began to set, the room felt as though it lit up with a bright light.

Once the greet was over, Perla asked, "So, what did you think of the meet-and-greet?"

"It was okay," I said.

"Okay?!" she said.

"Well, I didn't speak to many people," I said.

"Well, you were a little shy; that's normal," she said.

"So, it's my fault?" I snapped back.

"Oh, that's not what I meant."

"I'm sorry. I just... I'm not used to this, and I feel like it went horribly. If I can't even talk to the parents, how am I supposed to teach a class?"

Perla sat down at her desk and said, "You will do fine. Once you see the kids, everything will change."

I hoped she was right. "Well, are we gonna share a desk?" I asked.

She laughed and said, "No, your classroom is next to mine. It's just not ready yet."

"I have my own classroom? But I thought this was a combination thing?" I asked.

"It is, but you still have your own work space."

"Well, I haven't even decorated it, or have anything ready. Do I have to buy stuff?" I said.

"No, don't worry. I will help you. You helped me a lot with the supplies, and even though you thought you didn't do great, you did."

I leaned in and gave Perla a hug. It was the only way I could show her at that moment that her telling me I did great was what I needed today.

She hugged me back and said, "Well, thank you for your help. I'll call you soon to make sure you're ready the first day."

"Okay. Well, thank you!" I said as I left her classroom.

I walked down the long, quiet hallways of the brightly lit school. I could see other teachers in their classrooms, sorting away. Just as I was about to leave, I saw a board in the hall that read in neon bubble letters, "What's New!" I saw my introduction page pinned there and stood staring at my photo. I had my hair down, makeup on, and a big smile on my face.

Standing there, I felt a wet trickle down my leg. I looked down and saw what looked like a few drops of blood on the floor. I gasped, looked around my feet, and started to pat my legs to see if I could feel anything. *Am I bleeding?*

I thought. I took several steps back to see if it trailed, but it didn't.

I began to panic. I felt my breathing increase, and as I took more steps back, I walked inside a classroom during another teacher's meet-and-greet. There were three parents in the classroom. I looked at them and said, "I think I'm bleeding. Can someone please help me?" I was breathing heavily.

They walked over to me. I saw the teacher behind her desk stand up and grab paper towels. She approached me and said, "Dear, are you all right?"

I was leaning against the chalkboard and said, "I was walking, and I felt something. When I looked down, there was red… It was blood…blood drops…on the floor."

The parents just stood still, looking at me. The teacher walked out into the hall for a moment, came back inside, and said, "There's no blood, dear."

"No…yes, there is. It was right there on the floor."

"Do you need me to call someone?" she said.

I looked back at the parents and stayed just inside the doorway, glancing back and forth from the inside of the classroom to the white, clean floor. There was no blood there.

"I saw…I saw it" was all I could mutter.

The concern from the parents and teacher began to shift. I realized they were now taking steps back from me.

I looked at them and said, "I'm sorry."

I walked out and rushed to my car. I got inside and drove away. I knew I saw blood. I knew it was me. I knew somehow something was wrong, but I had no idea what happened. I kept trying to figure out how something could have just disappeared. I started to panic.

"What if they see my picture and recognize me and think I'm nuts? Did someone prank me? What is wrong with me?"

My breathing was now much faster. Once I got to the apartment, I rushed inside. I ran to the bathroom, and I began to check every inch of my body, my clothes, and my shoes. I didn't find anything.

Just then, I heard the front door open. Jason called out, "Laurie, I'm home!"

"Gonna shower!" I yelled back.

I ran quickly to turn on the water. I jumped inside while the water was still cold, slid down in the tub, and began to cry. When I felt the water get warmer, I turned my face upward into it and felt the little makeup I had on wash away. I sat there with my knees against my chest, trying to calm down.

"If it's back, I can't tell anyone...especially not Jason," I said out loud to myself.

* * * * *

Saturday morning, Jason woke me up with a cup of coffee. "Get dressed, hon, there're a few houses I wanted to look at today."

I stared at him from the bed and said, "What time is it?"

"Eight in the morning," he said as he checked his watch.

I sat up, grabbed my coffee, and took a sip. My stomach felt hollow; I could feel the heat of the coffee sink into the pit of my belly. I licked my lips and felt that I was beginning to salivate. I quickly stood up and headed to the bathroom. I barely made it before I suddenly felt my stomach bile rise up, and I threw up.

Jason rushed into the bathroom; he came over to me, held my hair back, lowered himself, and said, "Laurie, are you okay?"

I looked over at him and said, "Oh, Jason, no. Please don't look at me right now."

"Laurie, you just threw up. I wanna make sure you're okay?"

He helped me stand up, and I walked over to the sink. I washed my mouth and held the towel close to me, almost as if it were my own personal security blanket.

"Maybe the coffee was too strong?" he said.

I didn't want to tell him that this wasn't the first time I'd thrown up; it was just the first time he'd seen it. I smiled and tried to change the subject. "Um, are the houses you want to see open houses?"

He smiled and said, "Yeah, a few. I saw a few online, and I made a couple of appointments today. But if you're not feeling well, I can go."

"I'm fine," I said. I began to brush my hair and swept it to the side. I had dark circles under my eyes. I put concealer on, and when I looked up, I saw Jason had come close to me.

"You know, you have such beautiful blue eyes," he said.

"Stop," I said.

"It's true, but you always hide them behind your sunglasses."

"Jason, I've just…been a little tired."

"Oh, I never asked; how was it meeting all the parents?"

"I don't wanna talk about it right now. Just let me get ready, and we can go look at houses," I said.

He walked out of the bathroom, and I finished getting ready.

* * * * *

It was a nice day; the sun was out. I felt as if I hadn't really seen much of it. My skin was already fair, but after so long of hardly going out, I'd begun to get pale.

We began driving through a neighborhood that was near the apartment. The houses sat on a hill that overlooked the town. Jason pulled into the driveway of a two-story modern home; there were windows everywhere and a beautiful huge tree that sat on the side of the house. He opened the door to the house, which was a surprise; I'd expected to be greeted by someone who was showing the house. But the house was completely quiet.

I walked through the house as Jason started telling me things about the neighborhood. I wasn't really listening; I was in awe of the size of the home. The kitchen was very spacious, and the living room had large windows that had a great view of the backyard with a pool. I walked upstairs and into the hallway where all the bedrooms were. Jason was standing in the room at the end of the hall. I passed two other rooms and walked to where he was. I didn't say anything. I knew it was the master bedroom, and it was a very spacious room. The bathroom was also large, and through the bathroom was the closet.

"This closet is huge!" I said.

But Jason didn't say anything. He was just watching me. I walked out of the bedroom, and I saw him walking into one of the other rooms. "What do you think of the house?" he asked.

"It's huge," I said.

"Do you like it?" he asked.

"It's a nice house, Jason, but it has three bedrooms."

"Yes," he said.

"Well, what are we gonna do with all of this space?"

He was walking around in the room as he said, "Well, obviously that's our bedroom, and this could be my office, and the other room could be whatever we want."

"Like a gym?" I said as I walked into the spare bedroom.

"A gym?" Jason said unsure.

"A baby's room?" I said.

I heard Jason sarcastically giggle as he said, "A nursery?"

"Yes," I said.

"Laurie, you know I don't want kids," he said as he leaned in and gave me a kiss on the forehead.

He turned around and was almost out of the room when I said, "You don't want kids right now, but maybe one day you'll change your mind."

Jason stopped, turned to look at me, and said, "No, Laurie, you knew when you met me. I told you specifically that I don't want kids."

"Why?" I asked.

"I don't want to start a fight about it," he said.

"Why would it start a fight, Jason?"

"It's personal reasons, and I love you too much to hurt your feelings by discussing it further," he said.

"Jason, I know you don't want kids, but you never told me why," I said.

"I don't want to talk about why, Laurie," he said as he walked out of the room.

I stood in the empty room, looking around. I realized then that I'd never known how much I wanted a child until Jason told me he didn't want any. I walked down the stairs to see where he was.

Jason was leaning on the kitchen counter, and when he saw me, he said, "So?"

"So, what?" I said.

"Welcome home, Laurie, this is our house," he said with a grin.

"What? This is our home?" I asked.

"Yeah, I've been looking for a while, and when I saw this one, I knew I had to make an offer. It was too great a deal to pass up. I mean, it's perfect. It's in the same neighborhood where we are now, I'm close to my office, and you're close to work."

"So, you bought a house?" I said angrily.

"I bought our home, Laurie. I wanted to surprise you," he said.

"Well, I'm definitely surprised."

"I didn't think this would be your reaction," he said, puzzled.

"No, Jason, I love it. It's just…I wanted to be a part of the home-buying process."

He walked towards me and gave me a hug as he said, "How about you decorate the house? Make it a home."

"I can do that," I said.

"That a girl," he said.

"So, what are we gonna do with that extra bedroom?" I asked.

"How about we do that room last?" he said.

I didn't want to start a fight either. Instead, I closed my eyes and held Jason a moment longer before we left the house and headed back to the apartment.

Chapter 6

The apartment began to fill up with boxes again. It felt as if we'd just moved in yesterday, and here we were, moving out. I was doing most of the packing since Jason was at work, and we were going to be out of the apartment by next week. I didn't want to wait until the weekend for help from Jason, and I just wanted to be done with this already. I was so tired of packing, bubble wrapping, and shoving boxes aside to make space just to move around. I felt as if the apartment was starting to feel smaller than it already was. I was overwhelmed—another move, a house that I would decorate, and a new job starting soon.

I had woken up from a nap, the sun was down, and instead of making dinner, I decided to work on packing up the kitchen. I began to feel as if the room were starting to spin as I was writing "Kitchen" on one of the boxes. I put the cap back on the Sharpie and started to get up and walk towards the bathroom.

I stood there splashing water on my face. When I looked in the mirror, my face looked distorted, almost as if it were melting. I fell back and leaned against the wall. I slid down the wall and closed my eyes. I raised my wet hand with my eyes closed and brought it to my face. I was inhaling and exhaling quickly. I felt my right cheek, and it was warm to the touch and waxy, almost like a candle. I felt as though if I pressed my finger to my cheek, it would puncture my skin.

I yelled loudly and began to cry. I reached for the towel and buried my face in it. As I sat there yelling and panicking, I thought the worst. Just then, I heard the door slam and Jason run inside, yelling for me as I continued to scream. I could hear him trying to get through what seemed like a maze of boxes extending down the hall to the bathroom.

After a while, I could feel both of his hands grip my wrists as he tried to get me to calm down. I wasn't letting go of the towel because I was still screaming into it.

"Laurie, please calm down," he said loudly.

"No, my face! My face!" I yelled.

"What is wrong with your face?" he said.

"It's falling off!" I whimpered.

"What?" Jason said as he tried harder now to pull the towel away from my face.

"No! If you pull it off…my face will come off. I don't want you to see me like this," I said, still whimpering.

"Laurie, stop, please; just trust me," he said. I felt him bring me close to his chest.

With the towel still covering my face, I cried into it and could feel the tension from my wrists slowly begin to loosen my hands' hold on the towel. I put the towel down on my lap and cried into Jason's chest.

He held me tightly and let out a deep sigh as he pulled me away from his chest and said, "Laurie, you're fine. I'm looking at your face."

I looked up at him, shoved him aside, and crawled up to look at myself in the mirror. I was fine. I turned back to look at him and said, "No, you don't understand. My face was not right."

"What do you mean it wasn't right?" he said as he sat down on the bathroom floor, staring at me.

"I felt off, and I came to the bathroom to splash water on my face, and it was…it was coming off. It was…"

"Coming off?" he said.

"Yes."

"Laurie…" he said as he stood up and took off his suit jacket.

"Jason, I am not lying…please."

"Did you take—"

I could feel my blood boil, knowing what he was going to ask. It had nothing to do with my medication, and I knew that he would bring it up. "Yes! I am taking them, and it's not that at all!" I interrupted.

"It was just a question, Laurie, okay? I'm just trying to help," he said.

"Well, you're not!" I continued to shout.

Jason walked out of the room. I hated arguing with him, and I know he was trying to help, but I was so scared of whatever it was that just happened. I was mostly scared of not being able to keep my cool around Jason. I always felt as if I had everything under control with him, that he saw me a certain way, and now I wasn't so sure.

* * * * *

Jason didn't say much to me the next few days. He came home early from work the day of our move. The movers were there early and loaded the boxes onto a moving truck. Jason looked as if he had a lot on his mind, and I knew I was just adding to that.

After a while, he walked over to me with two keys and said, "I don't know how long all of this will be, but can you do me a favor and wait until they're done and then drop off our keys at the front office? Everything is good to go."

"Where are you going?" I asked.

"To the house. I'll meet you there when they're done," he said as he walked over to his car.

I could tell he didn't want to be around me, but I needed to tell him that I couldn't be alone. I just couldn't tell him why.

I walked back inside the apartment and watched as everything filled the moving truck. Box after box was leaving the apartment. I checked each room as it began to become more empty. I looked through all the cabinets and the drawers; I opened the closets, stood up on my tiptoes, and saw that there was nothing left that belonged to us. Finally, the last box was loaded. As I shut the front door and locked it, I told the movers to head to the house while I dropped off the apartment keys at the front office.

Jason sent me a text: *Where are you?*

I replied: *Leaving now.*

As I drove off after turning in the keys, I was relieved to not be in a small place anymore. I was looking forward to yet another fresh start, a place to call our own that had our name on it—well, Jason's name. I saw the movers were unloading as I pulled up to the house. I walked inside and saw Jason there directing everyone, telling them where to put what.

I stood there at the doorway and without a thought said, "Did I tell you that you look really handsome today?"

Jason looked at me seriously and said, "Laurie, we have company," as he glanced over at the movers.

"Oh, am I making you uncomfortable?" I said mockingly.

"No, but time and place, Laurie," he said.

"Well, this is our home, right?" I said sarcastically. I walked over to him and tried to give him a hug.

He stiffened and said, "Can we do this later?" He walked upstairs, holding a box that said, "Jason's Office."

The movers stared at me as they witnessed my own husband reject my silly flirtation. Then, they hurried back to the truck and tried to finish unloading.

I smiled as they came in and out with boxes. I started to feel as if I were in someone else's house, not even my own house; just the stuff was mine. I walked around as they unloaded the last of everything and went upstairs to find Jason sorting things in his office.

"Are they done?" he said as I stood in the doorway.

"Yeah, just now," I said.

He got up and walked past me to head downstairs.

I turned and stood at the rails, looking down as Jason handed the movers cash and they left. It was finally quiet, and I could focus on just us.

"Hungry?" Jason said as he started walking back upstairs.

I shook my head.

As he reached the top, he pulled me in for a hug and said, "Are you doing better?"

"I'm just a little uneasy," I said.

"You scared me, Laurie," he said as he looked down at me. Then, he walked over to our bedroom and sat on the unmade bed.

I sat next to him and said, "I don't know what's going on."

"Maybe you need a different medication?" he said.

"I don't know, Jason. I really want to stop taking them. Do you really think I still need that?"

He glared at me, almost as if I were a stranger, and said, "Laurie, you know how you are without your medication."

I looked down and said, "But I'm okay, Jason."

"No, Laurie...you need them. I can't ever see you the way you were again."

"Jason, I know something is off, but I can handle it."

"I think you need a different prescription. Maybe what happened the other day was some side effect to what you're taking," he said.

"Side effect?" I asked.

"Yeah, it can happen. The dosage is pretty high. Have you been experiencing anything else?"

I sighed and said, "No questions."

"Laurie, I'm asking as your husband, not as your doctor."

I looked at him, and I know I should have told him that I was tired, vomiting, and nauseous, but I lied and said, "Nothing else."

He patted the bed, indicating for me to walk over and sit next to him. He held my hand and said, "You will be fine."

I exhaled and lay down on the bed.

"Why don't you rest. I need to finish some things in the office."

I nodded and shut my eyes.

* * * * *

The days came and went. I was busier than ever with unpacking and trying to get everything ready for my first day of work, which was just days away now. I felt as if, even though everything was slowly coming out of boxes and being sorted, and the furniture was in our new home, I could still hear an echo. There were so many empty spots, empty wall niches and shelves, and the empty bedroom upstairs—it all began to haunt me.

I stood in the laundry room and waited for the last of the wash to be finished. I felt as if I had been washing and rewashing the more I unpacked. The noise of the washing machine and dishwasher was a constant. I heard the *ding* from the dryer that signaled the clothes were finally dry.

I opened the door and loaded the bin. I loved the warmth from the newly dry clothes, and I could smell the fresh linen. I closed my eyes and inhaled; then, I walked out of the laundry room and up the stairs.

As I passed the empty bedroom, something caught my eye. Jason was standing in the bedroom, staring out the window. I put the clothes down in the hall and walked to the bedroom door. He was frozen still, as if he was fixated on something. I stood at the threshold and said, "Jason?"

He didn't move.

I walked in and began to move closer to him. I put my hand out and was about to reach for him when I heard my phone ring. "I'll be back," I said. I walked out, grabbed the laundry bin, quickly placed it on the bed, and grabbed my phone. Perla was calling. "Hello?"

"Hi! Just wanted to see if you had any questions before your first day?" she said.

"Oh. No, I think I'm okay," I said. I started grabbing some clothes and began folding as Perla was talking to me about what to expect. "I'm looking forward to it," I said. As I hung up, I continued to fold clothes. I could feel the clamminess of my palms. I really was nervous to start work soon. I sat on the bed and called out to Jason, "You're home early."

He didn't respond.

I left him alone and finished the laundry. I crawled into bed when I was done and decided to take a nap.

A few hours passed, and I woke to the sound of the garage. I lay still and heard the garage close. Then, the door downstairs opened, and Jason walked in. I looked at the clock; it was 8:32 p.m. "Oh my gosh," I said as I wiped the drool from my face. I got out of bed and walked downstairs.

Jason was standing at the kitchen counter, looking through his phone.

"Hi," I said.

"Hi, hon," he said. "Were you asleep?"

"Yeah, I was tired. Did you go out and get dinner?" I asked.

"Yeah, I tried calling, but you didn't answer," he said.

"Oh, why didn't you wake me up before you left?"

"Wake you?" he said.

I walked to the fridge and grabbed some fruit as I asked, "Oh, by the way…what were you doing in the bedroom earlier?"

"Earlier when?" he asked.

"Earlier when I was doing laundry," I said.

"I don't know what you're talking about?"

"I was coming up the stairs. You were in the spare room, looking out the window?"

"No…I've been at work all day," he said.

"What?" I said. "Jason, stop. I saw you."

He scoffed and said, "Is something going on…again?"

"N-No, I-I just…" I stammered.

He walked over to his briefcase and began searching for something. He took out a small pill bottle, opened it, and said, "I've been meaning to give this to you. It'll help.

I tossed the other medication already, okay?" He held out his hand.

I grabbed the pill, then a bottle of water, and took the medicine.

"If you feel queasy, I can give you something else for that, okay?" he said.

I nodded my head. I started to feel as though perhaps Jason was right. I hated to admit it, but maybe there was a problem with my previous medication. "I just finally thought I found something that worked," I said.

"Hey, trial and error. Plus, you've been on that for a while now, so it's okay to find something else that will help you in ways that the other one didn't."

"So…you said if I felt queasy, that could be normal?"

"It could be, why?" he asked.

"Oh, no reason," I said.

He leaned in and said, "You know you can always talk to me…about anything, right?"

I shook my head.

"Why not?" he said as he put his finger on my chin.

"I want to tell you everything, Jason, but I don't want you to diagnose me if I confide in you."

He grabbed my hands and said, "How about we change the subject for now and go to bed?"

I smiled, and after that comment, I was hopeful that Jason was starting to see me as his wife, not his patient.

Chapter 7

My alarm buzzed at 6:15 a.m.; it was my official first day of work.

I went to the bathroom and saw that I had been spotting. I realized that I didn't even remember the last time that I had my period. So, I had to make a pit stop at the pharmacy before I went to work. *Great,* I thought, as I rushed to get ready.

I had planned to curl my hair and put on makeup for today, but, instead, I put my hair up in a bun with a pencil holding it all in place and applied a bit of light lipstick and blush. Then, I got dressed and headed downstairs.

Jason was already drinking his black coffee when he looked at me and said, "Wow, you okay?"

I paused and said, "Yeah, I just don't want to be late." I walked over to him and gave him a quick kiss.

He smiled and said, "Good luck! Call you later."

I smiled and headed to the garage. I was driving out of the neighborhood when I saw that just behind the nearby high school was the pharmacy. "Thank God!" I said out loud.

As I parked, I rushed inside. I headed to the aisle where all the pregnancy tests were, grabbed one, and rushed to the cash register. I could tell the cashier knew that I was in panic mode; she didn't even say a word to me as she placed the test in a bag and handed me the receipt. She gave me a smile as I grabbed the bag and headed out.

I was finally headed to work. Once I arrived, I parked in one of the teachers' parking spaces in the front of the building, placed the test in my bag, and walked towards the school, feeling the coolness of the fall breeze blow through my hair. I walked inside the school. It was still early, so I figured I could sneak away to the bathroom to take the test.

I went to the front office, checked my teacher's mailbox, and saw the key to my classroom, with a note attached that said, "Have a great first day!" It was signed by Chelsea Halls. I smiled as I read the card and grabbed the silver key taped to it.

Just then, I heard a familiar voice from the teachers' lounge. I peeked in and saw a few other teachers sitting there; some looked up at me and smiled, and others were talking amongst themselves.

"Hey, Laurie!" said Perla.

"Hey, Perla!" I said.

"Are you ready for your first day?" she asked, holding a cup of coffee.

"Well, I hope so!"

"If you need anything, let me know!" she said as she made her way out of the lounge.

I stood there for a moment and exhaled as I started towards my classroom. I could hear my heels clicking on the tile floor. Just as I looked to my left, I saw my name in big block letters, "MRS. BENKS' SECOND-GRADE CLASS." I unlocked the door and could smell the newly cleaned scent escape the room as I walked in. I turned on the bright lights, walked over to my desk, and placed my bag down. I opened it and took out the small place cards I'd made for each student.

As I went to each small desk and placed a name down, I started feeling sick. The on-and-off nausea was intense at times. This was the first day in a long time that I was up this early. I stared at the clock and saw I only had a few minutes before the students would be released from the cafeteria to go to their classrooms. I was starting to get nervous.

The loud bell rang, causing my head to pound for a moment. I could hear the students slowly walking down the hall. As they arrived and came in, they walked over to their desks, found their names, and sat down. They were so quiet. I'm sure they were just as nervous as I was.

"Good morning, students!" I said aloud.

"Good morning," a few muttered.

I stood in front of my desk and began to introduce myself. "My name is Laurie Benk. I just moved here from New York City a few months ago, with my husband, who is a psychiatrist in town. Does anybody know what a psychiatrist is?"

A student raised her hand.

"Yes!" I said as I pointed to her.

She stood up and said, "A psychiatrist is like a doctor, right?"

I nodded and said, "Very good!"

Another student raised his hand and said, "Do you have any kids, Mrs. Benk?"

I looked down and said, "No, I do not."

There was a moment of silence in the classroom. All of the students just sat still.

I looked around and said, "Let's all go around the classroom and introduce ourselves. I want you all to stand up, say your name, tell me where you are from, and if you want, you can tell me what your parents do!"

I remained standing, leaning against my desk, as I saw each student take turns telling me about themselves. Just as the last child sat down, I turned around, faced the board, and said, "Okay, everyone, we are going to start our reading now. I want all of you to turn to page two of your reading book and read to page six. When you are done, we will discuss what you read."

I sat down and grabbed the textbook. I got my highlighter and began to mark what I thought we could discuss. Just as I finished, I noticed many kids still with their noses in the books. I stared at my watch and realized that the time was going by rather quickly. It was already almost time for lunch.

"Okay, who wants to tell me what they thought of the story?"

We began the discussion, but moments later, I heard the lunch bell. All the kids slammed their books shut, grabbed their lunches, and lined up at the door.

I stood up and said, "Okay, kids, see you after lunch!"

I waved at them as they walked down the hall, following Perla, who was guiding the students to the cafeteria. I walked back inside and remembered that I had not packed a lunch because I was in a rush to go to the pharmacy.

"Oh, the test!" Just then, I realized it was still sitting in my bag. I grabbed the bottle of water on my desk and began to drink as much as I could before grabbing my bag and heading to the bathroom.

As I walked inside, I quickly took a peek to see if I was the only one in there. Thankfully, I was. I sat down in the stall, took the test, and held the stick as if it were gold. Determined to be very careful where I placed it while I cleaned myself up, I went over to the bathroom sink, grabbed a paper towel, and placed the test upon it as I washed my frigid hands. I started to pace back and forth. I could feel the sweat under my watchband; it had suddenly gotten tighter on my skin. I unclasped the gold-link chain and placed the watch on the counter.

I stared at myself in the mirror. "Hello, blue eyes," I said out loud to myself. I looked down and saw the loading symbol on the test still turning. It was so quiet in the bathroom. I could hear my heart beating in my chest and feel the beads of sweat dripping down from my neck. I started pacing again. My heels on the tile floor were starting to become louder and louder.

I could hear the seconds hand on the watch—*tick, tick, tick.* "C'mon...this shouldn't take this damn long," I said. I walked back up to the sink and looked down.

There it was, in bold letters—*PREGNANT.*

"Oh my God!" My heart was beating much faster now. Just as I started to feel an ounce of doubt, I realized I had unknowingly placed my hands on my stomach, already protecting what was mine.

I should be happy, right? I thought to myself.

Of course, I was happy. I was just scared. I realized that right at this moment I was the only one who knew this, and I wanted to keep it to myself. I didn't want to share it with anyone yet, not even my Jason. *Oh God, does that make me an awful person? I mean, he should know, right?*

As I stood there, I suddenly noticed I already had small dark circles under my eyes. My hair was a bit unkempt, and my white button-down shirt was slightly untucked from my black pantsuit. "Oh my, I look horrible."

Buzz.

"Oh Jesus!" My phone fell on the ground. I bent down to pick it up and saw Jason was calling. I cleared my throat, stood up, and answered, "Hello?"

"Hey, hon, I was just calling to give you a heads-up that I'm gonna be a little late today for dinner."

"Again?" I asked.

"Yeah, I have to meet a patient."

"Um, I guess I'll see you later?"

"Yeah, see you tonight."

As I hit End, I realized that I had no idea how I was going to tell him. Maybe show him the test? Take a picture of the test? I was walking back to my class with all of these thoughts rummaging through my head. I opened the class-room door, walked inside, and shut it. I needed to be still and silent for just a few moments longer. I sat at my desk, forefingers rubbing my temples. I could feel a headache coming on.

I stared at the clock. I had a few minutes before lunch was over. I took out my math book and had just started to write "Counting Coins" on the board when I heard the shriek of the lunch bell. I could hear the horde of little feet running through the halls, rushing to get to class. I walked over to the door, and as I opened it, I saw the small faces coming to my classroom.

"Hello, Mrs. B!" yelled one of my students as she strolled into class.

"Hello! How was lunch?"

"It was short!" said one of the other students.

I laughed, and as the last student walked in, I shut the door behind them.

"Okay, kids, let's get our math books out!"

I heard the moans and groans of the kids and realized that I really didn't want to teach this right now either. I smiled and said, "C'mon, kids, it's gonna be fun! We're learning about counting coins today!"

I walked over to my purse and started taking out the coins for the class. "Ah, here we have a nickel...and a quarter..."

As I stood there muttering to myself, from the corner of my eye, I saw Sophie, a student in my class. She walked up to me and stood staring for a moment before she tapped my hand and said, "Mrs. B?"

"Yes?"

"Are you okay?" she asked.

"Yes, of course, just getting the coins out of my purse."

"Oh, because your eyes look really red."

"Oh, Sophie, My eyes are red because I have allergies! It's windy outside today, and it's making my eyes watery. That's all." I smiled at her and saw a smile on her face now. Gosh, that was so easy—looking at her and telling her that I was okay, even though I wasn't.

As I was finishing up the lesson, the final bell of the day rang. I was shaking the coins around in my hands as I saw the students jump out of their seats and line up by the door. I dismissed them and waved goodbye. I walked over to put the coins back in my wallet and saw that I still had the test sitting in the pocket of my purse. I quickly zipped it and placed my head in my hands as I sat for a moment at my desk. I gagged from the smell of the rusty metal that lingered on my palms from the coins. I stood up, grabbed my bag, turned off the lights, and walked out, heading to my car.

As I was driving off, I could see all of the parents at the school, picking up their kids. Some were walking home, pushing baby strollers; other moms were running after their kids on the sidewalk, and even a few grandparents were picking up their grandkids. I wished that I had that. I just had Jason. As I felt the hollowness tug at me, I glanced down at my belly and realized that I wasn't alone anymore.

HONK!

"Oh!" I slammed on the brakes. I wasn't paying attention. Oh my God...I almost hit kids crossing the street. Not even a mom yet, and I was already failing at it.

The woman in the oncoming car, the one who honked at me, lowered her car window and yelled at me, "Really, lady? Pay attention!" and drove off.

Well, I just felt horrible. If I could sink further into my seat, I would. I was stuck in school traffic and could feel the glaring eyes of everyone in their cars. I turned up the volume on the radio as a distraction, even though that was absolutely what I did not need right then.

I needed to focus. Focus on the road, and focus on what I was going to say to Jason. I always had my radio tuned to the '90s station; it reminded me of better days, I suppose, of the days when I didn't have a care in the world.

As the school traffic cleared, I headed to get some food. A burger and fries would do.

* * * * *

Pulling into the garage, I noticed that Jason was home. "Great," I said out loud. *He said he was gonna be home late. Now what do I say?* I thought.

I walked in holding the bag of food behind my bag, hoping he didn't see that I opted to not cook tonight. He was standing in the kitchen on his phone, and he looked up as I entered. He was so good-looking. He stood in a navy-blue suit, his jet-black hair combed to the side, and whenever he would leave a few buttons unbuttoned, you could see the red-and-black skull tattoo on his chest peek through the shirt.

He smiled at me and said, "Oh, hi! How was your first day?" Then, he looked down at my bag of burger and fries and frowned just like Sophie today at school.

"Are you okay?"

"Y-Yes," I stammered.

"Since when are you hungry for a burger?"

I laughed. "Oh, Jason, it was a long day. I don't feel like cooking."

"You should've told me. I would've picked up something to go." He grabbed the bag out of my hands and threw it in the garbage.

"Well, thanks, there goes five dollars and sixty cents," I said sarcastically.

He laughed and said, "You'll thank me later. There's this great place that you would love off of Comos Street. I wanted to check it out."

I didn't want to go anywhere. I paused and asked, "Hey, what happened to your patient?"

"Oh, cancelled. C'mon let's go," he said.

"Jason, I really don't feel like going out. I don't feel well, and I'm so tired."

Jason looked at me and said, "You just need to head upstairs, change your shirt, and meet me in the car, okay?"

As Jason walked to the garage, he grabbed his phone. I could hear the clicking of the buttons as he texted.

I walked up the stairs and into our closet. My hands were clammy. I was unbuttoning my shirt, and the buttons kept slipping away from my fingers. I decided to rip off the shirt. As I did, small white buttons fell on the floor. I grabbed a blouse and rushed over to the mirror. I put on my dark-red lipstick, took out my now-messy bun, and started to head downstairs. Right when I reached the bottom, I stopped suddenly and realized I was out of breath. "Holy cow!" I said out loud.

As I walked out to the garage, I saw Jason sitting in his black sports car, staring down at his phone. The little light from the cell phone was bright enough that I saw a smile on his face. When I shut the door to the house, he looked up at me and grinned. As I got in the car, he turned to me and said, "You look great; let's go eat."

The speed of the car made me a little woozy. The neighborhood where we lived was very quiet. There weren't a lot of lights, and the neighbors seemed to keep to themselves. I reached down to grab Jason's hand.

He looked at me and said, "Something on your mind?"

I held his hand close to my face, kissed it, and shook my head. If he only knew.

* * * * *

When we pulled up to the restaurant, I unbuckled my seat belt and decided to leave my purse in the car. When I reached behind the driver's seat to place it down on the floorboard, I noticed a bouquet of flowers. I looked at Jason and said, "Flowers?"

He looked over at me and said, "For you." He leaned in to give me a kiss.

We got out of the car and headed inside the restaurant. Jason grabbed my hand, and we walked over to the host, who greeted us and asked, "Reservation?"

"Yes, under Jason Benk, for two."

"Oh, I didn't know you made a reservation?" I asked.

Jason's cheeks suddenly looked flushed. He leaned over to give me a kiss on my forehead and said, "Always a step ahead of you, hon."

I smiled as we walked to our table.

Jason pulled the chair out for me, and I looked up at him and smiled. As the waiter came by to take our order, Jason looked at me and said, "I'll have a glass of your Merlot, please. And my wife will have water tonight."

I smiled at Jason and looked at the waiter, who just nodded his head as he left our table.

"So, why the wine?"

Jason laughed and said, "Really? It was your first day at the school! I thought we would celebrate and spend some time together since I have to fly out tomorrow for a few days."

"Oh! That's right. I forgot you were leaving," I said.

"Aw, it's okay, hon. You can make it up to me when we get home," Jason said with a wink.

My stomach was already in knots, and I couldn't think about anything else right then. Especially sex. I looked at my glass of water and then glanced over at a table with two young women who were laughing and staring at Jason. A blonde and a redhead. The blonde was wearing a small black dress, while the redhead was wearing a black skirt and puffy purple blouse. They weren't shy at all about the fact that they were staring at a married man.

I started gulping my water down and realized that Jason was staring at me as I drank.

"Thirsty?"

I laughed and said, "Just got a little hot in here, that's all."

Our appetizer came to the table, and the strong smell of the calamari that Jason had ordered was so disgusting. He knew it was my favorite, but today I couldn't even stomach it. "This looks great," he said, grabbing a small plate to serve me. Jason spooned some of the appetizer onto the smaller plate and handed it to me.

For a moment as I stared at the calamari, I couldn't help but think how badly I wanted to run to the bathroom and throw up. I grabbed my ice-cold water and took a sip. I could feel the ice cubes on my lips and the water slide into my dry mouth. I didn't eat at all. I just stared at my plate, looked up, and watched as Jason was eating the calamari.

"You love calamari..." he said, confused.

I smiled nervously and said, "Jason, I've been telling you all evening I haven't been feeling well."

Jason dropped his fork and knife, wiped the side of his lips, and said, "I just wanted to do something nice for my wife."

I reached over to grab his hand, and he looked up at me as I said, "This is nice. I just really want to lay down. I'm sorry if I ruined our dinner."

He smiled, reached across the table, brushed his thumb on my cheek, and said, "I'll get the check."

As we sat there and waited for the check for our appetizer and drinks, the two women who had been staring at Jason were done with their meal and getting up to leave. I was relieved. As they passed our table, the blonde's purse brushed against Jason's shoulder.

"Oh, I'm so sorry!" she said and stood there waiting for Jason to react.

Jason looked up at her and said, "It's no problem."

Instead of leaving, she stared at the flowers on the table and asked, "What's the occasion?"

I looked up at the blonde and said, "My husband is romantic. I'm a lucky girl."

She didn't even look my way; her eyes never left Jason as sarcastically she said, "Isn't that nice?" She leaned into the redhead's ear and muttered something. Both women snickered as they walked away.

It had been a long time since I felt that I was being made fun of. I looked down at my hand and stared at my engagement ring as they walked off.

"Hey, don't let her get to you; she's clearly been drinking," Jason said with a smile.

I looked at him and smiled, and without even realizing, a tear fell from my eye.

"Are you crying?" Jason whispered. He almost looked embarrassed. He started to look around, trying to see if anyone else had noticed that I was teary.

"No, sorry. It's just been a day," I said.

Jason got up, walked to the host station, and pulled out his wallet. I guess I did embarrass him after all. He couldn't even sit with me at the table and wait for the check.

As I sat alone at the table, I looked around the restaurant. There were many couples. I caught myself staring at a family having dinner together. I saw how the mother was cutting up her daughter's spaghetti, and how the child was in awe of her mother, who was helping her. As the mother finished, the daughter laughed and started to eat. I smiled, trying to imagine that for us.

Just then, I caught Jason waving me down. I got up and walked towards him. I couldn't be happier to finally leave.

Once we were in the car, Jason rolled down the windows. The cool air that blew into my face felt so calming. I closed my eyes and inhaled the freshness of autumn.

Jason was looking at me as he put his hand on my thigh. "Are you hungry? You haven't eaten anything?" he said.

I turned to look at him and said, "I can just make myself a sandwich when I get home."

He said, "Or you can always pull out that burger and fries from the trash that you wanted so badly."

I felt a sting in my throat and glared at him as I said, "Jason!"

He looked at me again and said, "I'm kidding."

I took his hand off my thigh and turned to stare out the window, again trying to enjoy the cold air as we drove home.

Chapter 8

The next morning, I woke up alone in my bed. Jason had left without saying a word. Without even a goodbye kiss. I sat up in bed and realized that it was still very early for him to be gone already. The clock was flashing "6:51 a.m."

Why was I even up right then? My eyes still felt very heavy. My hair was a mess. I slouched down in bed and laid my head back down on the pillow. I reached over to grab Jason's pillow and pulled it close to me. I could smell his cologne; it was strong.

I swallowed a large gulp of saliva. The taste of my morning breath was thick in it as well, all mixed in as one. I opened my eyes, got up, and quickly ran to the bathroom, almost sliding as I rushed across the tile floor. I crouched down, quickly pulled my hair to the side, and threw up.

That's better, I thought.

I sat down on the cold floor and felt everything spinning for a moment. I really needed to see someone, but how could I go to a doctor without even telling Jason first? I was starting to become very paranoid. I felt as if I had a really bad stomach bug. Nausea was always present, even after I threw up. My senses were heightened, like that of a wolf. I looked like an animal—my hair was a mess, and my eyes were dark and gloomy. I could smell the sweat from my skin.

I got up and decided now would be a good time to take a nice, hot shower. Just before I stepped into the stall, I reached for the phone and called the school. I couldn't believe I was already calling in sick on my second day of work.

"Hi, it's Laurie, Laurie Benk," I said as the front office answered.

"Hello, Mrs. Benk, how are you this morning?"

"Not so great, I think I may have caught something. I'm nauseous, and I really need the rest," I said.

"Oh, okay, I will let Mrs. Guerrero know," she said.

"Great, thank you!" I said. I hung up and hoped the shower would make me feel a little better.

* * * * *

The rest of the day was pretty much a blur. I spent most of my time in bed. I hardly ate; saltine crackers and ice-cold water were the only things my body could handle. I lay in bed, in and out of sleep. It was almost midnight when I reached for my cell phone and sent a text to Perla: *Hey, I don't think I can come in tomorrow either. I have been in bed all day. Thank you for covering my class today.*

There was no reply. I figured she was probably already asleep and wouldn't see it until the morning. I felt horrible for asking for this favor from her, but she did say, if I needed anything, to let her know.

My nausea was so bad. I really didn't care about anything at that point, other than sleep. I shut my eyes and fell into a deep sleep.

I woke up and saw that it was 6:30 p.m. I had slept well into the next day and had done absolutely nothing. I sat up in bed and grabbed my almost-dead phone. I saw several missed calls from the school—8:45 a.m., 11:01 a.m., and finally 4:13 p.m.

I felt dizzy, I slid down in bed, and shut my eyes again.

* * * * *

I woke to the sound of the garage; it was 10:00 p.m. It must be Jason getting home from the airport. I pulled myself up and realized that he was two hours late; he had said his flight landed at 8:00 p.m.

I heard him walk up the stairs, and he saw me lying in bed. He was trying to be quiet, but once he saw that I was awake, his eyes widened, and he came closer to me, sat down on the bed next to me, and said, "Did I wake you?"

I smiled and said, "No, I haven't been doing so well. I have been in and out of sleep for a while now. Where were you?"

Jason looked down at me. His eyes looked darker in the pitch black of night, almost as if two small galaxies were staring into my soul.

"You know I can't tell, hon," he whispered.

"Work stuff, I know, but this late?" I said.

He nodded his head and leaned in to give me a kiss. I gave him a small peck on his lips, and I felt his lips linger on mine. He tilted his head to the side and leaned farther in to give me another kiss. As I felt his lips on mine once more, he suddenly stopped, looked at me, and said, "What's that smell?"

He wiped his mouth with his long shirt sleeve. Even though he had been traveling and was home late, I could tell that there wasn't a mark on his shirt. I could still smell the crisp linen scent on his clothes; he was always so perfect.

"Oh…well…I took a shower…" I replied.

He looked me up and down, took the large comforter off my warm body, and gently pulled me up from the bed. Once I was sitting facing him, he said, "You need a bath. C'mon, let me help you, okay?"

I smiled, and as I slowly stood up from the bed and wrapped my arms around him, I could smell the stench from my underarms. The lingering dried-sweat odor wafted into the air. I looked at Jason, hoping he wouldn't notice.

He let out a small cough, looked at me, and began to pace quicker towards the bathroom. He turned on the lights and let the hot water run. As I stood there, leaning against the countertop of the bathroom, I saw Jason slowly unbutton his sleeves and begin to roll his ironed shirt up towards his elbows. He took his black-leather shoes off, the black socks as well. He came over to me and reached out his hand. I straightened from the counter, and with all of my weight, I leaned forward to grab his hand. He smiled at me in a way that told me he knew I was at my most vulnerable right then. I lifted up my hands, and I could feel Jason pull my long pajama shirt over my head. I slid my underwear off rather quickly because I started to feel my skin shiver in the chilled air as the air conditioner turned on. Jason noticed and grabbed my hand to help me into the tub. I sat down in the tub and looked at him.

Jason smiled and said, "Okay, you need to relax and unwind. I think you might have caught a bug or something from one of your students."

I looked at him and said, "You're probably right." I leaned my head back and shut my eyes. Jason had no idea that I hadn't been at work these past two days.

I heard Jason leave the bathroom. From the bedroom, he called out, "I'll be back in a few!"

The door was open, and as much as I tried to relax, I was fixated on what Jason was doing. I could hear him unzipping his suitcase. He was coming in and out of the bathroom, walking through to get to the closet with a pile of laundry. He didn't even glance at me as he walked by. I knew he could tell that I was staring at him, but perhaps he thought that if he gave me an ounce of attention, it would break the calmness with which he thought he'd left me.

I sat up in the tub and decided to bathe myself. I could feel the soapsuds gently wipe away everything off my body. I grabbed Jason's forest-scented shampoo. It smelled of pines. I closed my eyes as I rinsed off. Just as I pulled the drain, I looked down and saw the water was now murky. I hadn't realized how dirty I was; it was almost as if I never showered yesterday. I got up quickly before Jason could see. As I wrapped the towel around my body, I walked over to the mirror and wiped the steam off. I stared at myself as I wrung out the water from my hair.

Suddenly, I felt Jason standing behind me. "Hello there, blue eyes," he said as he stared at our reflection. He smelled my hair and said, "Since when do you use my shampoo?"

I turned my head to the side and said, "Since it relaxes me."

He leaned in, gave me a kiss, and said, "Well, whatever helps, I suppose." He walked towards the tub, turned the shower on, and started to undress. As he got in and closed the curtain, I began to dry off.

I walked downstairs after putting on pajamas, grabbed a glass, and filled it with mostly ice and a little water. The cubes on my lips made my head buzz for a moment; it was so cold. I felt a sense of relief after my hot bath. I stood there in the kitchen for a moment, drinking my ice water, when I heard Jason coming down the stairs.

He was wearing black boxers and a black T-shirt. He grabbed a bottle of water from the pantry and stood next to me. After looking down at my glass, he said, "You're gonna catch a cold."

I looked at him and lied as I said, "I just don't know why I feel so off."

Jason opened the medicine cabinet and started rummaging through pill bottles. Many were prescriptions with names that were definitely not store-bought. Being a psychiatrist had its perks. Jason had done many clinical studies and tests; that had led to opportunities for him to conduct trials for new medications.

Pulling a small white bottle from the back of the cabinet, he opened it, put two little white, round pills on the counter, and said, "Here, take these…it'll make you feel better."

I just stared at him.

He said, "Don't worry, it doesn't interfere with what you're taking. I mean, it's already two in the morning, and you have work tomorrow. If not, I can go with you to the doctor instead of work. Your choice."

My choice? I thought to myself.

He grabbed my hand and placed the two pills in it.

"What is it, anyway?" I asked.

He closed my hand and said, "I would never give you anything that would hurt you."

I looked down at the pills, tilted my head back, popped them in my mouth, and swallowed. I reached for my ice water and drank it quickly. I could feel the pills slide down my throat.

"Now, let's go to bed."

I nodded and followed him up the stairs. As I got in our bed, Jason pulled the sheets over my arms. As he lay across from me, I stared into his eyes.

He said, "Good night, Laurie."

* * * * *

I woke up that morning to Jason sitting on the edge of my side of the bed. He was already dressed for work. The sunlight was peeking in through the windows; the clock read, "7:15 a.m." I quickly sat up.

Jason said, "Wow, wow, relax, hon."

"I'm gonna be late!" I said, jumping out of bed.

"Well, I see the meds worked, then?" Jason said as I ran into our closet. He stood up.

I looked back at him and wondered how he got ready so quickly, without even waking me up at all. His hair was combed; he wore a grey suit and his black lace-up shoes. I could smell his cologne in the closet; he must've just sprayed it. It radiated through the air; every breath was an inhale of my husband. I smiled. I noticed that I did feel much better.

I grabbed my black pencil skirt and my red blouse, quickly got dressed. Put my black flats on and swooped my hair up into another bun. I applied a tad of blush on my pale cheeks and some lip gloss. As I rushed out of the bathroom and down the stairs, I saw Jason drinking his black coffee and watching the morning news.

Jason looked at me as I quickly paced through the kitchen, making my lunch for the day. He frowned and said, "What are you making?"

"Oh, a PB and J…and an apple!" I said.

He laughed and said, "That's very typical of you."

I stopped and said, "What do you mean?"

He put his mug down, turned to me, and said, "Just, maybe that's why you haven't been feeling so well lately. You don't eat enough."

I grabbed a small bag of pretzels, looked at him as I did, and said, "There, better?"

He smirked and said, "Okay, well, that's my cue to head to work." He grabbed his cell, wallet, and keys. Without a kiss goodbye, he turned to me as he grabbed the handle to the garage door and said, "See you for dinner," and walked out.

Right then, I didn't have time to think about anything else except that I was going to be late for work. I could just imagine my students sitting in the classroom without me there. I better hurry now or it would be me in the principal's office today.

* * * * *

I sat in traffic; the clock read, "8:54 a.m." I was so late. School started at 8:15 a.m. I knew I was going to be in trouble.

When I finally pulled into the parking lot, it was 9:07 a.m. I rushed out of my car and ran into the building. When I reached my classroom, I saw Perla sitting at my desk and teaching my students and hers. They were in the middle of reading when she saw me and said to the kids, "Keep reading. I'll be right back, everyone."

She came up to me and said, "Laurie, can we talk?"

I took a step back into the hallway and said, "Of course."

She shut the door and said, "Are you okay?"

"I'm here! I'm just late. I thought I caught a bug or something, but I feel a lot better today," I said.

"Okay, well just text me, okay? I have to explain to the parents why they didn't see you out front today for pickup."

I looked down. I didn't know what to say, other than "It won't happen again."

With a kind smile, she walked back into the classroom. I followed her inside, and she said, "Okay, all of my kids, back to our room!"

The students groaned. I think they liked mingling with the other kids. As I made my way to my desk, my students cheered and said, "Morning, Mrs. B!"

I felt better just with that. The rush to get here was paid off by hearing how glad they were to see me.

Perla smiled as she left and shut the door behind her.

"Good morning, kids! I am so sorry about this morning."

Tyler, a student in my classroom, said, "Oh, I was late this morning too!"

I laughed at his honesty. "Okay, kids, let's pick up on our reading where Mrs. Guerrero left off."

* * * * *

The day seemed so long. By the time the bell rang for the end of the day, I was wiped. As I headed home, I got a call from Jason.

"Hey, hon, how was your day?"

"Good, How is your day?" I said.

"It's good so far. I should be getting off around six today."

I sighed. I was so nervous to be around Jason.

"So, what are you gonna make for dinner?" he said.

"Oh, I hadn't even thought about it." I laughed. Food was the last thing on my mind right now. Just as he mentioned dinner, I realized I hadn't even eaten my lunch.

"Um, salmon sounds great," Jason said.

I let out a heavy sigh, and Jason was quiet on the phone. "Okay, I'll go to the store and get some," I said.

"Great, see you tonight."

Once I got to the store, I started walking right to the fish section in the back. I walked down the aisle with all the chips and drinks. I grabbed a small bag of chips and began munching. I stood in the aisle and realized that cheesy chips tasted delicious. I finished every last bite, crumbled the bag, and tossed it. I was licking my fingers as I headed down to get the salmon. I could smell the strong odor of the fresh fish. I could see all of them laid out on a bed of ice. I saw the two men behind the counter, handling the fish, cutting them, wrapping them up, weighing them, and handing them out to the customers.

I walked up to one of the men and said, "I'll have the salmon, please." As I got closer to the counter, I pulled my blouse up, covering my nose. The man stopped for a moment and was staring at me. I tried to act as normal as possible, letting go of my blouse and smiling. I held my breath as I watched him filet the salmon, wrap it, weigh it, and hand it to me. I grabbed it from his hands and rushed towards the aisle, as far away from the fish as I could get, before I exhaled loudly. I couldn't stand the smell. I walked to the aisle where the candles were. I looked at the names of the scents—Lavender and Fresh Linen—and finally saw some red candles labeled Ruby Red. I picked one up and closed my eyes; it smelled like a spa. I grabbed a couple of candles and left the store.

* * * * *

I finally got home, unwrapped the salmon, and immediately gagged. Thank God for the candles. I lit them all and dimmed the lights. I felt relaxed enough to cook the meal that I was not at all craving. I licked my lips and could still taste a bit of chips. I got a glass of ice-cold water and began to cook. Once the salmon was cooking, the smell wasn't so bad. The rawness of it was slowly fading. I bent down to grab a bowl for the salad, and when I turned, Jason was standing in the kitchen.

"Well, hello there," he said.

I jumped and said, "Hey, Jason. Gosh, you scared me!" I walked over to him and kissed him as he wrapped his arms around me. I fell into his arms and welcomed his embrace. His tie smelled of cigarette smoke and his cologne. I looked up at him and kissed his chin.

He looked down at me and said, "You look great. Feeling better?"

I looked at him and said, "Yeah, a little bit better today."

Jason gazed around the kitchen and said, "Nice candles."

I realized just then that the red candles and the dim lights were giving off the vibe that I was trying to be romantic. I smiled, and without acknowledging his remark, I turned to the stove and said, "Dinner's ready!"

Jason walked over to the table, sat down, and said, "This looks delicious."

I looked at him and said, "It's what you said you wanted."

Walking towards the table with the salmon, my hands were trembling as I got closer to Jason. He was staring at me the entire time with a sly smile. He looked as though he was happy to see that I was more myself. I sat down and stared at the salmon.

Jason devoured the fish and salad. He looked as if he was starving for more than just food. I was so hungry too; my stomach was mumbling, and I put my hand on it to hold it. I looked down at my belly. I realized I needed to feed my baby. I looked up at Jason and took a bite of the salmon. It didn't taste bad; it was actually good.

Once we were done eating, I put the dishes in the sink. Just as I was about to wash, I felt Jason's hands from behind me, and he held me in a warm embrace again. He stood there and said, "Don't worry about the dishes right now, hon." He turned the faucet off and grabbed my hand. We walked up the stairs and into the bathroom. Jason undressed, and then he started to remove my clothes as well. He looked at me and said, "Laurie, you are so beautiful," as I was covering my body with my hands.

I saw him turn on the water in the shower. He walked into the stall and turned to me, holding out his hand. I walked towards him and grabbed his hand. We were in the shower together now, and he started to slowly kiss me. I felt the weight of the last few days washing away. Moments like this was how Jason and I usually were. I opened my eyes and felt the heat in my body rise. I told myself it was just because of the moment, but no, I felt as if I was starting to get weaker and weaker. Everything was starting to slowly fade. I could feel my breathing begin to become more rapid, my heart beating faster. I couldn't tell if I was sweating or if it was just the heat from the water that was engulfing me. My hair was stuck to my back. I turned to face the water and closed my eyes as it splashed my face.

Jason held me so tight. The steam from the shower was making the whole bathroom a blurred fog. I could feel Jason's hands on my belly. I looked down at his hands and pulled them away from my stomach. I could feel his arms tense as he tried to put his hands on my stomach again, and I quickly turned to face him. He smiled at me, and as he leaned in for a kiss, I felt my stomach begin to grumble. I turned my head as I slowly started to taste the acidity of bile work its way up my esophagus and—*blurt*—out it came. All over Jason.

He stopped for a moment and took a step back. He looked down at his body covered in my vomit and asked, "Are you okay?"

I wiped my mouth and reached for Jason. I wanted him to wash off the mess.

He looked at me more intensely and said, "Laurie?"

I could feel myself leaning back against the shower. I watched him take a few steps closer and rinse himself off. I heard him scoff and turn the shower off. He grabbed the towel and stepped out. I hadn't moved from my spot against the shower wall. I was staring at him, waiting to see what he was going to say.

"Laurie, what's going on?" he said. He turned to me.

I was staring at him and said, "I just haven't been feeling like myself lately."

Jason started to pace back and forth in the bathroom. "You've been saying you haven't been yourself lately for a while now...you aren't physically sick. I just saw you eat dinner; you went to work; you don't have a fever! I mean—"

I cut him off and said, "I need time, okay?"

"Time?" Jason said.

I came out of the shower, and I walked towards him. I didn't grab a towel. I was completely nude. "Yes, time."

"Time from me?" he asked.

I could feel my eyes begin to swell up with tears. I couldn't control myself anymore. I fell to the floor and began to cry.

Jason looked down at me. He stared at me for a few minutes before he came down to my level, and with his forefinger, he lifted my chin and said, "I think it's more than that, Laurie."

I wiped my tears away and looked up at him. "What the hell is that supposed to mean?" I said.

"Laurie, I can tell when someone is having a mental break," he said condescendingly.

"I am not your patient anymore, Jason. I'm your wife! How many times do I have to tell you!" I yelled.

Jason stood up and said, "Laurie, as my former patient, I know you through and through. This isn't you right now, okay?"

"I know myself. I don't need help. I just need time."

"You're on the damn floor, crying for no reason!" he said loudly. He took a step back and leaned against the bathroom counter.

I could feel the water from my hair turn cold now. It was starting to slide down my back, just as my tears were sliding down my cheeks. I felt as if Jason was looking at me as though I was a puzzle he was trying to piece together. I could tell he was frustrated with me.

"Just talk to me..." Jason said as he looked down and reached for my hands.

I looked up at him and said, "I think that there is something missing..."

"Missing? With us?" Jason looked confused, his eyes now looking into mine.

I looked into his eyes and thought that if I slowly unfolded the truth, maybe he would accept it.

"Did you mean what you said? You really never want a baby?"

Jason's eyebrows furrowed, his face was frozen for a moment, and then I saw his smile lines crease as he let out a laugh.

That was not what I expected. "Why the hell are you laughing?" I said, my voice slightly raised now. I wiped my face and grabbed my damp hair. I twisted it, feeling the water wring out as I waited for him to respond.

He said, "Laurie, really, a baby?"

I tried to shift closer to him, but he slid away from me, and I felt his hand untangle from mine.

"I don't know what to think. I'm confused, Laurie. Like I said, you haven't been yourself for a while now."

I looked down and said, "So, what are you saying?"

"I think I'm the one that needs time," he said. Jason stood up and walked out of the bedroom.

I sat motionless on the floor and started to cry again. I realized how ridiculous I looked to him. I felt as if his image of me had changed within a matter of minutes. One moment, he wanted to be close to me as husband and wife; the next, he walked out on me. He must've thought this had to do with him.

I got up, went to the bedroom, pulled the sheets down, and even though I was not fully dried, climbed into bed. I wanted to feel a sense of security. I was so tired from crying; I felt so faint from the shower. I just needed to rest before I went after Jason. If I could just shut my eyes for a few moments and find the energy, then I could go talk to him.

Chapter 9

I was in such a deep slumber that I felt as though my skin had cemented itself to the bed. There was a small, dark puddle from my damp body and hair. I hadn't moved at all throughout the night, and I also felt drool on the side of my face. My throat was dry; I'd clearly slept with my mouth wide open. I looked at the clock; it was 10:02 a.m. I was so late for work. Even though I'd just woken up, I was still so tired. I just wanted to go back to sleep, but I realized that I'd left things horribly last night with Jason.

I got out of bed and walked around the bedroom, looking for where he might be. I walked downstairs, opened the garage door, and saw that his car wasn't there. I was alone. I went back upstairs and found that I had left my phone in my purse last night; it was completely dead. I plugged it in and rushed to the shower. It was the quickest shower I'd ever taken.

My hair was soaked, and I put it up in a wet bun. I changed into a navy-blue dress and leopard flats. I ran downstairs, pulled my phone off the charger, and headed to my car. I sat in the car and checked my phone. I saw two missed calls from the school and one missed call from Jason.

I was so nervous about listening to the voice mail he had left. I sat still and held my breath as I heard his voice; he sounded so upset. "Hey, Laurie, I know it's early, but I wanted to call before you went into work. I don't know what is going on, and I feel like I have done what I can, and you keep shutting me out. I need to focus on work. We will talk soon."

I must've replayed that message a hundred times just to hear his voice. I tried calling him, but there was no answer.

I called Perla, and she answered almost immediately, seeing as how it was time for lunch. She also didn't sound too happy with me. "Laurie! Where are you?"

"I'm sorry. I'll explain everything soon. I just have a lot going on right now. I'm headed to work now." I hung up before she could reply.

This day was horrible. I closed the garage and headed off to work.

* * * * *

Once I got there, Perla was very short with me. She hardly maintained eye contact and was rushing to her class to get ready for the kids to come back in from lunch break.

"Please don't be upset. I can explain," I said.

"You keep saying that, Laurie. We all have things going on, but you have to start taking work seriously." She turned away from me and left.

I felt as if, no matter what I did or whom I spoke to, I was being scolded. I know I should tell someone about what was going on, but I felt stuck in a corner. I wasn't sure whom I could open up to right now.

I sat at my desk and waited for the bell to ring. I had about ten minutes left, and I was going to utilize them. I stood up and started to write the lesson for the day on the board. Just as I did, I began to feel light-headed. The lights in the classroom began to flicker. The bell rang; lunch was over.

The students were starting to come inside, and it was almost as if I could smell them before they even came into the classroom. The halls wreaked of sweat and dirt. I stood at my desk, waiting to see the expressions of the kids.

When they saw me, they said, "Oh, Mrs. B! Where is Mrs. G?"

I frowned for a moment. "Oh, she went back to her classroom with her students," I said.

"But she said we were gonna watch a movie!" another student called out.

"Oh, did she now? Well, no, we are going to take a pop quiz!" I felt I had to do something to make up for the fact that I was behind with my own students, and in all honesty, I needed something to grade.

As I handed out the math quiz to my students, I sat down and stared at all of them holding their pencils, ready for my quiz.

"Okay, begin!" I said.

I sat at my desk and could hear the ticking of the wall clock. If I listened closely, I could hear the lead from the pencils scratching against the paper as the students wrote. I sat upright, but then felt myself start to hunch over. I clasped my hands, and I leaned my chin on them.

The next thing I knew, everything suddenly went dark. Before I knew it, I had dozed off in class.

* * * * *

I felt a hard nudge on my shoulder, and as I opened my eyes, I looked up and saw that it was Chelsea and Perla. My classroom was completely empty.

What just happened? How did I not hear a classroom full of students leave?

"Mrs. Benk, we need to talk," said Chelsea as she pulled a chair up to my desk.

Perla did the same.

"We have had several worried parents who have stated that their students have gone home, telling them that their teacher is not there in the mornings, and that Mrs. Guerrero has had to take over completely due to your absence here at work, more than once."

"I-I c-can ex-explain…" I stammered.

"Please do," she said angrily.

"I have been dealing with a lot of things lately," I said.

"Yes, Mrs. Guerrero told me that you seemed to have a lot on your mind. However, it doesn't mean that you can be absent from work without notifying anyone," she said.

"Yes, I know. That wasn't very responsible of me. I've just been so exhausted and a little loopy."

They turned, glanced at each other, and then looked at me. They probably thought I sounded crazy right then.

"Well, isn't your husband a psychiatrist? Perhaps he can help," said Chelsea.

"No, not with this… I'm…I'm pregnant," I said.

Just as the words left my lips, I felt more nervous than before, when no one knew anything. Now, two people knew, and Jason was not one of them.

"Oh, well. Congratulations!" said Perla. They were smiling at me, but also looked confused because I wasn't smiling back.

"I've been having a difficult pregnancy. I have been so tired, have lost a lot of sleep, and have no appetite at all. I've been nauseous, and I want to come to work, but I can hardly pull myself out of bed. I will do better," I said.

Chelsea looked down and said, "Well, why don't we do this? Why don't you take some time off? I've already made arrangements for a substitute to fill in, and I'll call you soon to see where you're at?"

"What?" I was confused. "Am I getting let go?"

"Laurie, you have been late two days in a row, and you fell asleep in class! Mrs. Guerrero cannot continue to watch double the amount of students, and parents are starting to ask questions."

I froze. I realized that there was no way that I was going to win this one. "Okay, I'm sorry," I said quietly. "I understand."

Chelsea and Perla stood up and walked out of the class-room.

I sat in my chair and finally saw the time; it was 3:30 p.m. I pulled out my phone and typed in the search engine: *pregnancy and fatigue*. Apparently, it was much more common than I thought. I'm sure it was just a normal side effect of the whole pregnancy.

I looked down, put my hand on my belly, and for the first time, spoke to my little baby, "Hey in there, I know you are growing, but you are really kicking my butt." I giggled. "I hope you're okay." I stood up and heard my stomach growl.

As I walked out of my classroom, I turned to take one last look before I left. I shut the door and headed out. I needed to eat, and since Jason wasn't going to come home, I figured now would be just as good a time as ever to grab that burger and fries. This time, he couldn't trash it.

* * * * *

After I pulled in the driveway, I stepped out of the car and walked inside. The house was quiet. The dishes from last night were still in the sink and smelled of fish. Nothing was cleaned up or put away. I put my purse down and went upstairs. I made my way to the closet and began to undress. I put my pajamas on and walked over to the sink in my bathroom to wash my face. Just as I grabbed the face wash, I noticed that Jason's toothbrush was gone.

He really did leave? I thought. Was I so exhausted that I was tuned out from the world around me? I began to fear the worst. What if I was in such a deep sleep, and someone broke into the house; or the alarm went off, and I didn't hear it?

I splashed the warm water on my face, and with it, splashed my thoughts away. I couldn't think like that right now. I headed downstairs, poured myself ice-cold water, turned to the burger and fries I'd picked up, and began to scarf down my food. It tasted so delicious, better than any thirty-dollar filet mignon. As I finished the last bite, I got struck with fatigue again.

I managed to stand up, walk up the stairs, and crash into my bed. I went facedown into my pillow and started to cover myself with a blanket. This was the best part of the day, the only sense of warmth that I felt in my life right now. It was just enough for me to doze off.

* * * * *

I had no idea what time it was. For a moment, I thought I must've woken up early; it was dark out. I looked at the clock, and it was 7:40 p.m. What?! I had slept well into the next night again?

I got out of bed. I felt nauseous. I checked my phone, and there was not one missed phone call or text message. I put it down and got a sudden craving for ice cream. I went downstairs, grabbed the vanilla ice cream from the freezer, and started eating.

I stopped and realized that something must be wrong. I was stuck in this horrendous routine. Ice-cold drinks only, light-headedness, exhaustion, and vomiting. I knew that if I were to go to the doctor, they would probably just laugh and say that all of these were normal symptoms of pregnancy.

I was digging again into the ice cream when I suddenly heard a buzz. I stopped eating and was surrounded by silence. Then, the vibration and buzz of my phone began again and got louder and louder. I slowly walked up the stairs and saw my phone on the nightstand. It stopped buzzing.

I rushed over to see who it was; it was Jason. Oh no! I missed his call. I sat down and tried to call him back, but there was no answer. I couldn't help but think maybe it was an accidental call, or maybe he changed his mind and didn't want to talk to me after all. I peeked out the window to see if maybe he was coming home, but didn't see his car.

Just as I stood there on my tiptoes, trying to see beyond the horizon of the night sky, I felt a pain in my stomach. I hunched over, ran to the bathroom, and threw up again. I wiped my face with some tissue and stood up. I walked over to the bed and got in. I felt that the only thing to make the days go quicker would be if I just never got out of bed. I felt the tears start to fall from my eyes. I shut my eyes tightly and dug my head into the pillow.

* * * * *

I woke up to the sound of rain. I lay in bed and reached for my phone. I called Jason, but still no answer. I didn't have the courage to leave a voice mail. I needed to actually talk to him.

Instead, I called Perla, and I didn't even know why. I had no one—no friends, nothing. Just coworkers.

She answered and sounded as if I'd just woken her up. I hadn't even checked the time before I called her. "Laurie, are you okay?" she said sleepily.

"Yeah, I'm sorry. I just…I'm all alone," I said as my voice cracked while I was trying not to cry again.

"Well, I can come by your house after work? Is that okay?" she said.

"Yes, please stop by," I said.

"Okay, Laurie, get some sleep."

As I hung up, I looked at the time on my phone—5:12 a.m. I was lying down facing the window and watched as the drops of rain hit the glass, accompanied by a flash of lightning and a roar of thunder.

Just then, I felt something in my belly. A kick? What was that? There was no way that I could already feel a kick this soon? I assumed I was in the early stages of pregnancy, but I really didn't even know how far along I was.

I reached over to grab my phone and searched: *How early can you feel a baby kick?* So many different articles came up. As I scrolled down, I saw something that caught my eye—"as early as eighteen weeks." If that was the case, that could mean I was a little over four months along.

I lay in bed, wondering if I was further than that? I remembered everything being a bit of a blur after the wedding. I felt so strange for trying to remember the last time I even had my period, but the last time I could remember was right before the wedding.

"Does that even make sense? How does someone forget their period?" I was talking out loud to myself, hoping to try to remember, but my mind was blank.

As the rain started hitting the window harder, I found myself scrolling through my phone. Just as I did, I saw that Jason had sent me a text message. He was definitely up early.

Jason: *I forgot to tell you. I filled a prescription for your nausea. Please take them.*

I didn't reply. I knew he could see that I'd read the text, but I just decided to put my phone on the nightstand and close my eyes.

Chapter 10

I was standing in line at the pharmacy in my pajama pants, T-shirt, and oversized sunglasses, with my hair in a messy bun, as I waited to pick up my prescription that Jason had called in. I approached the counter.

The pharmacist was very cheery when greeting me and said, "Good morning!"

"Hello!" I said.

"Well, well, are you here for pickup or drop-off?"

"Pickup," I said.

"Okay. Name?"

"Um, Laurie Benk," I said as I strummed my fingers on the counter.

"Oh now, that's a good one!" he replied.

I was confused. I stopped and said, "Excuse me?"

"Benk, you said?"

"Yes."

He stopped to look at the computer as I placed my ID on the counter. His entire demeanor changed as he said, "Well, Mrs. Benk, I'll be right back with your prescription."

I stood staring at him as he quickly walked to the back, then returned to me, and said, "Looks like you have a zero balance. Have a great day."

Before I could even say "you too," he had already walked away. *That was weird,* I thought to myself.

I headed out to my car, sat there, and ripped open the small, stapled bag. I read the instructions to "take two a day with milk or food." I didn't even know how to pronounce the name.

I picked up my phone, took a picture of the pill bottle, and sent it to Jason, texting: *Got it. What's it for again?*

Within a matter of seconds, he replied: *Trust me. It will help you.*

That was it? He could be so frustrating.

I headed back home and decided to make some breakfast. I really needed to try to start eating.

* * * * *

"What is in the fridge?" I said out loud as I opened the refrigerator doors. "Strawberries, eggs, and yogurt. That sounds good enough." I cracked the eggs, whipped them in a bowl, and cut the fresh strawberries as I took small bites from the yogurt and cooked. Once everything was ready, I grabbed the small plate of eggs and strawberries and sat down at the table. It was so quiet. I looked around, and I felt so lonely. Just as these thoughts crowded my head, I could hear my stomach rumble.

"I hear you in there," I said as I looked down and smiled.

When I finished my breakfast, I walked over to the sink and started to rinse off the pile of dishes and load the dishwasher. I grabbed the new pills and took one, made my way upstairs, and walked down the hall to where our bedrooms were. I walked inside the empty bedroom and sat down in the center. I looked around, almost as if I were seeing it for the very first time, and decided that while I was home, I could redecorate. I had ideas of maybe a home gym or a guest room.

Then, suddenly, my heart began to beat quicker as a thought came into my mind. *I could decorate this room into a nursery!* I grinned at the thought. I finally found the perfect way to tell Jason that I was pregnant.

I got up and began pacing around the house. As I looked around at the plain white walls, I saw in the corner of the rooms the small boxes that I had yet to find a place for, and then I came across our wedding album sitting next to a pile of empty frames on our coffee table. I sat down on the couch and pulled the album onto my lap. I opened it and immediately smiled. Pictures of our wedding cake, the guests, the party, Jason's father giving a toast, and me in my dress. The album was never ending. They were all photos of Jason's family, and I was alone in those of me. I slouched down, and just as I got a bit more comfortable, propped my head on the couch pillow and drifted off to sleep.

As I slept, I began to dream. I could feel my body diving into the memory of how Jason and I met.

* * * * *

I remember standing in front of the mirror, staring at myself. That day, I was wearing eyeliner, blush, and lipstick. My blonde hair was down and straight. I had on grey sweatpants and a simple tank top. I was in a rough place then.

The moment I walked into Jason's office and saw him in his beige suit, I remember regretting not putting a little more effort into my outfit. He looked so handsome that day. As we shook hands, he smiled at me and ushered me to sit down. I remember looking at him and not really paying attention to what he was saying or the questions he was asking me.

"Huh?" I said to him.

He looked down at the glass coffee table in his office and said, "Let's try again. Try to relax and just talk to me, okay?"

I sat back on his black-leather sofa and found it difficult to relax. I remember the more I opened up, the more I would start to show more emotion. Until in one session, I cried through most of it. I hardly said a word. He let me cry in his office; there was no consoling, nothing at all from him. I just remember him handing me a tissue box. I cried and cried that day.

Suddenly, my memory shifted to when I would purposely make my appointments with him, enter his office, and jump into his arms.

He would laugh and say, "My favorite hour."

I would laugh and begin to kiss him.

My dream shifted to a horrible fight we had. The day I told him I didn't want to see him professionally anymore, but solely as his girlfriend, and he said no. He was going to break up with me because he felt that as my psychiatrist, he was not truly helping me by dating me.

I went to his office and had a complete meltdown. I was crying, throwing things on the floor, and breaking a few figurines that sat on his desk. I remember turning around and smashing with my hand a photo he had of us on his desk. I was so angry that I didn't even realize how bloody my hand was.

I heard Jason yelling my name to make me stop. "Laurie!" he shouted over and over.

I didn't respond, as if Laurie wasn't even my name.

Just as my dream was shifting, I realized the noises from my dream were starting to become muted, and I heard a very loud knock.

*****

I awoke suddenly and realized that what felt like five minutes of sleep was actually several hours. I sat up and heard the knock again; it was coming from the front door.

I didn't even bother looking through the peephole. I opened the door, and I was happy to see it was Perla. "Hi!" I said as I stepped aside so she could walk in.

"Hi, Laurie," she said as she stepped inside.

"How are you?" I asked as we walked inside the kitchen.

"Good, good. You have a beautiful house," she said.

I turned to her and said, "Thank you."

"Laurie, I don't know you very well, but I am worried about you. I know we see each other at work, and I am happy you and I are talking, but is something going on? Do you need someone to talk to?"

I grabbed two glasses and filled them with water. As I handed her one, I stood across from her in the kitchen and said, "To be honest, I don't have anyone to talk to. I don't want a professional to hear me, if that's what you are hinting at. I just need a friend."

She paused and came close to me. She took my hand and said, "Okay, then as your new friend, I want to tell you that I am concerned for you."

I could feel my hands begin to tremble as she held them. I walked over to the kitchen table and sat down.

She came over, sat down, and said, "I know you said you're pregnant, and I'm really happy for you. But you also said you were having a hard time?"

I nodded my head.

She said, "It can be hard. Some people get very sick, and some people don't feel anything at all."

I knew it was difficult for her to converse with me. She hardly knew me and was trying to give me advice about my pregnancy.

"Can I ask you something?" she said.

"Yes," I said.

"Does your husband know?"

I paused and stuttered, "N-n-no-o."

"Why not?" she asked.

"He doesn't want kids," I said.

"*Ay, Dios mio,*" she said as she pulled her hands away from mine. Perla stood up, grabbed her glass of water, and began to drink it. She looked at me as she placed her glass down and said, "Well, what do you think you would do if he didn't want the baby?"

I looked at her, and without a thought, I said, "I would leave."

Her eyes widened. I'm sure that wasn't what she thought I was going to say.

"You really think that your husband didn't think that one day you would have a family?"

I shook my head.

She walked over to me and said, "Then, you need to show your husband where you stand. You are carrying his child, and he needs to know that you are ready, whether he is or not."

She was right. I needed to show Jason that this was the best thing for us. "Well, I had planned to turn the spare bedroom upstairs into a nursery," I said.

"Yes! Do it! And if you want, I'll go shopping with you," Perla said.

"Really?"

She laughed and said, "Yes, I know great stores here in town to help you, and I promise I won't tell anyone anything, okay? Not until you are ready."

I smiled at her and said, "Thank you."

"Okay, so I have to ask? Have you gone to the doctor?"

"Not yet. I don't even know how far along I am. But the other night when I was lying in bed, I swear I felt the baby move," I said.

"Oh my, you must be in your second trimester!" she said.

She reached in her back pocket, grabbed her cell phone, started searching through it, and said, "I know this great doctor. He is a little far, in town. Do you want his number?"

I nodded my head, reached for my cell phone, and handed it to her.

"Go ahead and put his number in my phone. I'll call to make an appointment," I said.

Just as she handed me back the phone, I looked down and saw "Dr. William Burtley" on the screen. I put my phone away.

Perla asked, "Are you taking your prenatals?"

I laughed and said, "No. I need to."

She turned to me and said, "I know you feel sick, but you need to take care of yourself. I'm sure everything you're feeling is part of it."

"You think so?" I asked.

She looked at the clock on the stove and said, "Oh, I better get going. I have to be up early for work."

As she walked to the front door, I said, "Perla, I just want to apologize for how we started. Thank you for helping me with my class and now this." I opened the front door.

Before she left, she said, "Laurie, I'm just happy you trusted me enough to tell me what really was going on." She smiled. "I'll call you, okay?"

As Perla walked away, she waved, and I waved back. I shut the door and let out a sigh of relief. Even though I knew Jason and I were not talking, and we weren't in the best place right now with our relationship, at least I wasn't doing this alone anymore.

Chapter 11

The next few days came and went. It was finally the weekend, and I hadn't heard from anyone. I knew Jason would take a while to want to talk, especially with his work schedule. But I was hoping for at least a text.

I got up early Saturday morning. I wanted to try to do something. As I walked to the bathroom and started to brush my teeth, I heard a *ding* from my phone. I quickly spit out the toothpaste and rushed to my nightstand. "Jason!" I said out loud.

Instead, it was a text from Perla: *Good morning. Are you feeling okay today?*

I was glad to hear from her. I replied: *A little better today, thanks.* I sat on the edge of the bed, waiting for her reply.

She finally said: *Are you busy today? I was thinking I could take you to the store I told you about.*

I responded: *No plans, what time do you wanna go?*

She replied: *How about in an hour?*

I texted: *Okay, why don't you come by, and we can go together.*

I put my phone down on my nightstand and walked over to the bathroom. I finished washing my face and decided to go *au naturel* today. Besides, I could just wear my sunglasses. I walked over to my closet and started looking through my clothes. As I was putting on my jeans, I felt that they were snug around the waist. Usually, I would be discouraged, but I was oddly happy. I knew that my body was changing, my belly was growing, and as I slid off my dark jeans, I grabbed my sweat pants and put them on. *Much better*, I thought. I wanted to be comfortable from now on—no more fancy Laurie. I grabbed a plain T-shirt and slid it on.

As I was walking out of my closet, I passed by my jewelry box. I stopped and opened the top case. I saw all the expensive bracelets, earrings, watches, and necklaces that just lay there. I didn't remember the last time I wore any of it. I opened the bottom drawer of the jewelry box, where I placed my engagement ring and my wedding band. That was the only jewelry I wore now. As I grabbed the two rings, I closed the drawer and made my way downstairs.

Once I reached the kitchen, I grabbed bread and decided to eat some buttered toast with my usual ice water. I also took my daily dose of medications and could feel my body shift as I adjusted to whatever new medication Jason thought I needed. He knew I trusted him; he always knew how to make me feel better. I just hoped that whatever I was taking was okay for my pregnancy.

As the toast popped up, I started eating. I turned on the small kitchen-countertop TV and listened to the morning news. I used it really just for background noise. It was too quiet with just me in this big house.

I heard my phone ringing and saw a text from Perla: *Hey, on my way.*

I replied: *Okay.*

I put the plate in the sink and turned off the TV. I walked over to get my purse and opened my wallet, making sure I had all the credit cards I needed. Just then, my doorbell rang. I opened the door, and Perla stood there with a welcoming smile.

"Ready?" she said.

I closed the door behind me and locked it. As I got in Perla's car, I turned to her and said, "I'm so excited to check this store out, but before we go, do you think we can make a pit stop at the ATM? If I buy anything, Jason will see the statement, and it'll be a dead giveaway."

Perla stilled for a moment and then just said, "Of course."

Once we got to the ATM, I got out as Perla waited in her car. I had no idea how much anything would be for babies, but I figured I would need quite a bit of money. I started thinking quickly about what a crib, stroller, diaper bag, diapers, and so on would cost. I had no idea what to even take out. The next thing I knew, I entered "5,000" in the custom bar for withdrawal. As the money came out, I grabbed the wad of cash and just hoped that Jason wouldn't check the account anytime soon.

I got back in Perla's car and shoved the money in my wallet. It wouldn't zip shut.

Perla sat there staring at me and said, "Okay, I think you are ready." She laughed as we drove out of the parking lot.

* * * * *

Once we got to the store, I could see from the window there were many beautiful baby items. I gazed at the displays of cribs, strollers, and clothes hanging on small mannequins.

We stepped inside and were greeted by a young woman who said, "Welcome! Is there anything I can help you with?"

Perla said, "My friend is pregnant. She is buying items from scratch for her nursery. Can you help us tell her what she will need?"

The woman's eyes lit up; she knew that we were about to be her new favorite customers. She went behind the counter and handed us what she called a New-Mommy Checklist. On it, there was a list of items, which she had in her store, that new moms had bought. I looked down and realized the items were listed by category—from furniture, to accessories, to clothing.

Perla looked at me and said, "Are you doing okay?"

I looked at her and said, "Oh, I'm just a little over-whelmed." I knew I didn't have to get everything today, but I wanted to get as much as possible.

I looked at the woman in the store and said, "Okay, I guess it's time to start shopping."

We went through the list. Anything that wasn't in stock at the store would be sent to my house, but I ended up getting a lot of items. Clothes, stroller, diapers, breast pump, bottles, and the list went on and on. The woman and the other employee helped to carry everything to Perla's trunk. We'd spent several hours there.

As I got in the car, my stomach was beginning to groan.

"Oh, you must be hungry!" said Perla.

I laughed and said, "I guess I am."

"What do you feel like?" she asked.

I turned to her and said, "How about a sandwich?"

Perla said, "I think I know just the place around here."

We ended up going to a mom-and-pop-style restaurant; they were known for their hamburgers, but also had simple foods like sandwiches. When we got there, we sat down, and I could feel my eyes getting heavy after all the shopping.

"You look like you want to pass out," Perla said.

"Today was the first day in a long time that I have been out on my feet. It must've caught up with me," I said. I looked around, and there weren't many people in the restaurant.

Perla started to tell me about all the wonderful things to do in Colorado, places to see, and then she shifted the conversation to me and asked, "So, what is New York like?"

"New York is great. There is a lot to do. If you aren't careful, you can get lost in a big city like that." I laughed.

But Perla cleared her throat and said, "I have been wanting to ask you a question, but I know it might be personal."

I leaned in a little closer and said, "That's okay; ask away."

"How come you don't want to tell your husband that you are pregnant, but you told me? And we barely know each other."

"Oh well, it's kind of a long story," I said.

She quickly said, "I don't mind."

I knew she was curious. She was diving into my life and letting me lean on her; maybe I could tell her what was going on.

"Um, well, I met Jason because I made an appointment with him. I was in a really dark place in my life, and I needed help."

"What kind of help?" she asked.

"Jason diagnosed me with schizophrenia. I was starting to get disconnected from reality."

"Oh," Perla said.

"I was referred to Jason because he did a new clinical trial in New York for people who were having hallucinations," I said.

"Did he end up helping you?" she asked.

"Well, yes and no. I was on medication, and I was doing much better. But then I started to flirt with Jason. I don't know how to explain it. I couldn't stay away, and it got complicated."

"Complicated?" she asked.

"Yes, he didn't want anyone to know that he was dating his patient who was doing a clinical trial and showing results. He thought people in the field would think I would say I was okay only because I was dating him, when in fact I was okay. He didn't want to lose his credibility."

"He was worried about his reputation?" she asked.

"I guess you could say that." I sighed.

"Are you still taking medication for that?" she asked.

"No," I quickly replied. I didn't want to tell her that I was taking anything. "A big reason we moved here was because he wanted a fresh start. He wanted to be in a town where no one knew who we were, where we could be a couple and just be ourselves," I said.

"But you all got married, and usually married couples do have kids," she said.

"Yes, but Jason doesn't want kids. I've always known that."

"But you do?" she asked.

I nodded.

"This is why you never date your doctor," she said.

I looked at her and said, "I would really appreciate it if this stayed between us, if that's okay?"

"Of course," Perla said.

It was nice to finally find someone to talk to about things. Someone who wasn't biased. Maybe I hadn't known Perla for a long time, but it was easier to talk to her, knowing she didn't know a lot about me. I was being vulnerable; it was something I hadn't done with anyone except Jason.

As we finished our lunch, Perla looked up at me and said, "I think I should get you home; you need to rest."

I smiled, and although I was having a good time being out, I couldn't keep my eyes open any longer. I wanted to crawl into bed so badly.

The drive home was nice, and I started to doze in the car.

A while later, I heard Perla say, "Laurie, you're home."

For a moment, I pictured New York. But as I opened my eyes and saw the two-story home, I sighed. I loved my home; I just didn't like coming home alone. I got out of the car.

Perla insisted on taking everything inside. She didn't want me to lift any bags or anything heavy. As she dropped off the last bag, she said, "Okay, I better head home now, but I'm gonna call you and check up on you later, okay?"

I nodded and said, "Thank you, Perla."

She leaned in and gave me a hug. I could feel that it was genuine. As she left, I shut the door. I was too tired to put any of the baby stuff upstairs in the room.

I walked upstairs and undressed. I was completely nude. I noticed the more tired I was, the colder I became. I crawled into bed, wrapped the blanket around me, and started to fall asleep holding my belly.

Just as I began to drift off, I felt a small kick. I looked down and said, "Hey, in there...I can feel you." I was so happy to feel my baby.

* * * * *

The next morning, all I could think about was Jason. I grabbed my phone as I lay in bed and sent him a text: *I don't know when you are coming home, but please let me know. I am still figuring a few things out. We need to be on the same page here.*

I got out of bed and started to slowly carry upstairs to the nursery what I'd gotten at the store. It took me a long while to do; I made sure to walk slowly and not overload myself. I shut the door of the room and put my hair in a ponytail.

When I heard the buzz from my cell phone, I scurried to my bedroom and saw that Jason was calling. I answered, "Hello?"

"Hey, Laurie, do you have a minute to talk?" he said.

I sat down on the bed and said, "Yeah, what's going on?"

I could hear Jason sigh. "I'm in New York. I'm at my parents' house right now," he said.

"You went to New York? I thought you said the clinicals were in Chicago?" I asked.

"Laurie, I decided to come here after Chicago. Did you forget that I had a life here?" he said defensively.

"A life there? But it was your idea to move to Colorado, Jason. You wanted to start somewhere fresh for both of us!" I could hear my tone getting louder and louder.

"I didn't want anyone finding out I married my patient!" he shouted back.

"What are you saying? That you're ashamed of us?"

"Laurie, I have been putting my work on the back burner, and you know how I felt about getting married right away. But I did it because I love you."

"What are you trying to say, Jason?" I asked.

"I'm just saying that you need to learn to start taking care of yourself and not be so dependent on me. Ever since we got to Colorado, something is always wrong."

"That is not true!" I said. I could feel my eyes starting to fill with tears. I didn't want him to hear me cry and try to turn this around and say I was being more unstable.

It seemed that he knew me too well. Even over the phone, he could always sense when something was wrong. "Laurie, this is what I mean. You are so emotional lately. You need to let me be there to help you and tell me what is really going on with you."

"So, you want to help me, but not be here for me as my husband? That doesn't make sense, Jason," I said as tears fell down my face.

"Laurie, look, you know you haven't been yourself. Just promise me you'll continue your meds. I'll call and check in on you, but right now you need some time to find your-self, apart from me, okay?"

"Jason, I'm not crying because of that. Look, there's something you don't know, okay?" I said. I figured this could be the opportunity to tell him that I was pregnant.

"What do you mean, Laurie?" he said.

"I have a lot of emotions because my life is changing. I should say that our lives are about to change."

"Laurie, what are you trying to tell me?" he said sternly.

"The other day, I found—"

Jason cut me off, "Hold on, Laurie. I'm getting a call… Let me call you right back."

Before I could say okay, the line went dead.

I sat on the bed, crying as I held my cell phone. I didn't want to have to tell him over the phone that he was going to be a dad. I wanted to tell him in person; I wanted to see his reaction. I was now more scared than before to tell him anything. I was so angry with him. If he felt that I needed time to figure myself out, I would show him that I found out that I'm about to be a mom, and that was my main focus above everything else.

I stood up and walked to the empty bedroom. I saw the piles of bags from the baby store, the stroller that still had zip ties all around it, a baby tub, and several bottles and pacifiers. I sat on the floor and started taking everything out one by one. I made piles for everything—the clothes in one, the kitchen stuff in another. I grabbed a pair of scissors and started cutting off all the tags from the white onesies. I grabbed the pile of baby blankets, clothes, small hats, and mittens and threw them all in the washing machine. I started hand-washing all of the bottles, pacifiers, and breast pump.

As the day was coming to an end, I was almost finished with organizing everything. The laundry was done, and

I had set aside all of the folded clothes and blankets in the laundry room.

Just then, my phone rang again; it was Jason.

"Hello?"

"Laurie, I got caught up. What were you gonna say?" he asked.

"Oh, I…um…I don't remember, Jason. I have a lot on my mind also," I said looking down at my belly.

"Have you been feeling better? No more nausea?" he asked.

"I'm fine," I said.

"Well, you don't sound fine."

"Oh? Well, how am I supposed to sound after my husband told me that he doesn't want to come home to his wife?!" I exclaimed.

"Laurie, I do want to come home. I just don't know when, okay?"

"So, you aren't coming anytime soon?" I asked.

"No," he said. We were both quiet on the phone until Jason broke the silence and said, "I need to go."

"Jason, just…call me when you decide to come home." I hung up. I wanted him to know that I was upset. I was tired of waiting for him.

I didn't want him to know that I missed him. I wanted him to miss me.

Chapter 12

I was in the home improvement store to buy some paint for the nursery. I had to do it before the rest of the furniture arrived. I walked into the paint aisle and was staring at the different pinks and blues. I wish I knew what I was having. My eyes strayed to the yellows, tans, and greys.

I finally decided to be cliché and look at the yellow swatches. I chose a color that was called Lemon Meringue. It was a soft yellow with a white hue to it. I bought the paint, the brushes, and everything else I needed to get the project going.

As I walked up to the cash register, the cashier said, "Project, huh?"

I laughed and said, "Yeah, I'm painting my baby's nursery."

"Oh, you and your husband?" she said as she looked down at my hand and glanced at my wedding ring.

"Just me," I replied.

She smiled as she finished ringing up the items and handed me the receipt.

* * * * *

Once I got home, I started prepping everything to begin to paint. I walked inside our closet and grabbed one of Jason's pajama shirts. I put on some shorts, and they wouldn't button. My belly was growing every day; I was starting to show now. I walked out of the closet and headed to the nursery. I put on the gloves, opened the paint, and began to pour it in the tin pan. I grabbed the paint roller and ran it through the paint. I walked up to the wall and began to roll the paint onto it, covering the plain white wall. It was quiet as I was painting. All I could hear was the wetness of the paint as it smacked the wall.

I began to envision what Jason's reaction would be when he came home and saw this. I kept imagining that he would walk through the front door, completely unaware of what was upstairs. I would tell him to close his eyes as we approached the nursery door. I would open the door, turn on the lights, and he would gasp, look around the room, turn to me, and say, "You did this?"

And I would smile and say, "Yes."

He would come towards me and give me a kiss. He would say, "I finally understand why you were so sick, why you were so emotional." And the best thing he would say was "I'm sorry."

I blinked quickly as I caught myself staring at the paint on the wall. I could only hope that that was what would happen, but deep down I knew that he wasn't going to react that way.

* * * * *

It was time for me to go to bed by the time I finished painting. The fumes of the paint had started to give me a headache. I turned the fan on and walked out of the room. I left the door open to air it out.

I walked across the hall to my bedroom and looked at myself in the mirror. I laughed as I saw small yellow splatters all over me. I walked over to the shower, undressed, and walked in. I looked down and saw the yellow water go down the drain. It was mesmerizing to me, to see everything wash away. I could feel the tension from my body release as I rinsed off the soap and shampoo.

I stepped out, wrapped myself in a towel, and glanced at myself in the mirror as I started to dry my hair. My arm was sore from all the painting; I could barely put my shirt on. I might have overdone it. I walked over to the bed, turned off the lamp, and fell into bed.

Just as I started to shut my eyes, I heard the sound of a baby crying. I shifted in bed and could still hear it, almost as if it was outside. I sat up in bed and looked around the dark room. I still could hear the crying. It wasn't outside; it was much closer. I got up but stood still; then, I took a few steps towards my bedroom door. The crying was much closer now. The house was pitch black, but I didn't turn any lights on. I took the first step into the hallway, and I could hear the sound of a small baby continuing to cry.

"I hear you," I called out into the darkness.

I walked over to the nursery and switched on the lights. Just then, the crying stopped. I searched the room. The paint smell was still pungent. Nothing was there, but I didn't feel alone.

"I need to sleep," I said aloud.

I walked back to my bedroom, turned the lamp on, and looked down at my belly as I said, "Was that you in there?"

I looked up, almost waiting to hear a sound again, but this time there was nothing.

"I hear you, baby. Mama's here."

As I lay in bed, I held my belly and fell asleep.

* * * * *

A month had gone by, and everything was still the same. I spent most of my days in bed, ate very little throughout the day, got up to shower, and went back to bed. Perla would check on me every now and then; she stopped by often to drop off food. She would tell me that I needed to make sure I was eating, especially now that I was eating for two. Most of the time, the food was thrown in the trash; I never ended up eating it.

I hadn't heard from Jason, and I missed him so much. I sent him text messages telling him I missed him and that I loved him, but he never responded to any of them.

I was sitting at the kitchen table when Perla called.

"Hello?"

"Laurie, hey, how are you?" she asked.

"Good, just doing the same thing I do every day," I said.

"I've been meaning to ask you, have you ever heard anything back from the principal about when you can come back to work?" she asked.

"I haven't really thought about it. I don't know if I want to go back this year," I said.

"Oh. Well, maybe you can set up a meeting or something just to give them a heads-up," she said.

She was right. I wanted to leave the door open for work in the future, but, right now, I didn't want to go back to work. I was still so tired all the time. Even though I was back on my medication, I felt as if everything was still the same, except for the nausea.

"You're right. I'll call and set up a meeting to see what to do," I said. As I hung up, I scrolled through my contacts list on my phone until I saw Chelsea Halls. I was so nervous to push the Call button.

"Hello, this is Chelsea Halls speaking; how can I help you?" she said as she answered her phone.

"Hi, this is Laurie, Laurie Benk," I said.

"Laurie, hi! How are you?" she said.

"I just wanted to call you to see how everything was working out with the substitute?"

"Mrs. Jenkins. She's wonderful," she said.

To be honest, it wasn't what I wanted to hear. "I just wanted to apologize for the way I left things. I know I never called you back, and I never heard from you either, but I have been having a really tough pregnancy. I was hoping to come back sometime soon," I said.

"Well, I would be lying to you if I said that the students didn't miss you. Mrs. Guerrero put in a good word for you."

"Oh, okay. Well, I appreciate that from Mrs. Guerrero, and I do miss the kids," I said.

"Well, I think that maybe we can try this again next year? I want to keep you on staff just in case we need you as a substitute for Mrs. Jenkins. I would like to be able to contact you, if that's okay?" she said.

"I would really like that," I said.

"Okay, great. Well, we do offer paid maternity leave. If I could just have a note from your doctor saying that you are cleared to return to work, that would be great. Since you stated you were having some issues..."she said.

"Yes, I wasn't feeling that great, but I can get a note..." I hesitated as I thought about how I would get one. I hadn't even seen a doctor yet.

"Great. Well, you know where I am, so just swing by, and I'll put your file in for review for the next school year."

"Thank you," I said.

"Thank you for calling!" she said.

At least that was taken care of. I just needed a piece of paper from a doctor, and I would be good to go.

I ended up calling Perla back to tell her the news. "Hey, Perla!"

"Laurie, hey, are you okay?" she asked.

"Oh, I'm fine. I just wanted to tell you that I called Chelsea. She told me that I can be on the schedule for next year, and a sub if they need me for this year. Isn't that great news?"

"Oh, that's great, Laurie!" she said.

"I just wanted to thank you; she mentioned you put in a good word for me."

"Hey, it's not a problem. We all go through some things, right?"

I smiled and said, "There's just one thing. I need to bring in a letter from a doctor stating that I am cleared to come back to work, seeing as how I left things with me not feeling so great."

"That's a problem?" she asked.

"Perla, I haven't seen a doctor."

"What?! Laurie, you have to get checked," she said.

"I don't know any doctors in town. I haven't even bothered to check. To be honest, I'm just so tired. I never want to go out, and I've been working on the nursery."

"You're still feeling tired? Are you sure that's normal?" she asked.

"I don't know," I said.

"Have you called Dr. Burtley's office?"

"Who?" I said.

"Dr. William Burtley, the doctor I told you about? I gave you his number," she said.

I had completely forgotten that she'd given me his number. "Oh, that's right. I haven't called. I'll call now and see if he can see me soon. There has to be a reason why I'm so tired all the time and barely have an appetite," I said.

"Well, let me know, okay?" she said.

"Thanks, I'll let you know how it goes when I go."

* * * * *

I felt as though it was the first time in a long time that I was being productive with my day, outside of my bubble of being home all the time. I looked at my phone and stared at Dr. William Burtley's phone number. I don't know why I was nervous to call, why I was anxious about seeing a doctor. I knew I had to, but I also knew, deep down, that being this tired wasn't normal.

I finally called, and a friendly woman answered the phone, "Hello, this is Dr. Burtley's office; how can I help you?"

"Hi, my name is Laurie, and I wanted to call to make an appointment."

"Okay, ma'am, are you currently pregnant?" she asked.

"Yes."

"How far along?"

"I'm not sure."

"Okay, I can have you come in Thursday at 2:00 p.m. Is that okay?"

"Yes," I said.

"Okay, see you then!"

* * * * *

The days went by slowly. I was in bed most of the time. I snacked on crackers and made very little dinner, which at times didn't stay down. I was at the point with my nausea that I was tempted to give up food altogether if it meant I wouldn't throw up anymore, but I knew I couldn't do that. My energy was very low. I would get tired just from walking to the bathroom and back to bed.

The house was always dark. I never turned on any lights or opened the windows. I didn't like turning on the TV or music while I was by myself; I felt as though I would miss the sound of Jason coming home.

* * * * *

Wednesday night, I felt as if I could hardly sleep. I went through my purse and made sure I had what they said I needed.

"Okay, license, insurance card... Oh, I don't have that!" I didn't have an insurance card because it had been a while since I'd even gone to a doctor. "Where would it be?" I said out loud.

Suddenly, my eyes wandered, looking down the hall; I was staring at Jason's office. I hadn't gone in there this entire time he was gone; I'd almost forgotten about it. I thought maybe Jason would have the insurance card stored away somewhere, and I wasn't about to ask him where he kept it. I figured I would go search for it myself.

I slowly made my way to his office and opened the door. I left the door open as I walked inside. I sat at his desk and started to open the top desk drawer. I could hear the *screech* of the drawer and saw pens and pencils neatly organized.

Nothing there.

As I shut it and went to the middle drawer, I saw notes that were written in gibberish. I could hardly read what Jason had written on pages and pages of a notepad. I turned the pages, and a few words caught my eye. I didn't think too much about it. I knew that it had to do with his work, and I didn't want to read something that would make me overthink. I already had enough on my mind. I closed that drawer and opened another.

I was frustrated because in the bottom drawer was a small chest that was locked. It sounded like something was jiggling around in it, but I couldn't find the key. I had a feeling that it was probably some pills, but who knew why it was locked away. I felt so dumb thinking I would find the insurance card, and even dumber for looking through Jason's things. He was so private about his work life. I felt guilty, but I couldn't help myself.

As I was making sure everything was closed, I saw in the trash a small piece of paper in Jason's handwriting—"182 days." I didn't understand what it meant. The note was scribbled through and tossed.

I walked out of the office and quietly shut the door. Although I was home alone, I felt as if I still had to keep quiet, especially after looking through Jason's office. I walked back to the bedroom, got in bed, and tried to get some sleep.

I hated that I was so unprepared for my appointment.

Chapter 13

I woke up feeling as if I'd hardly slept. I got out of bed and must've brushed my teeth twice due to my nerves. I started brushing out my hair and put it up. My anxiety must've started to set in because I felt as if I was warm. My cheeks were flushed. I sighed as I walked inside the closet to see what I was going to wear. I looked at my side of the closet, and everything looked as if it was a size too small. I tried to put on my jeans and a shirt, but they didn't fit.

Great, I thought as I put my jeans away.

I walked to Jason's side of the closet and decided I would wear a pair of his gym pants and a long hoodie. I looked in the mirror before I walked downstairs and felt as if I looked bigger. I sure felt bigger.

I got in my car and typed in the address of the doctor's office. "Forty-two minutes away!" I said out loud to myself, hoping not to get lost. I had no idea where anything was in this town. I was nervous to venture out.

Perla kept calling me. She knew my appointment was today, but I didn't want to answer just yet. I wanted to be clear in my own head before I spoke about anything. Deep down, I wished that I could call Jason and that I could be meeting him at the doctor's office, but, instead, I was doing this by myself.

It was a long drive. I got lost along the way. After a couple of wrong turns, I was finally on the right path. I started seeing more doctors' offices, and then I finally saw a sign that said, "Dr. William Burtley, Women's Health Center." I pulled into the parking lot and grabbed my bag as I got out of the car and walked into the clinic.

I saw a few women sitting in the waiting room. Some were there by themselves, others with their husbands, and most looked heavily pregnant. I felt as though they were all looking at me as I walked inside and headed to the receptionist.

"Hello, I have an appointment at 2:00 p.m."

"Hello, ma'am, new patient?"

"Yes," I said.

"Okay, I will need you to fill out these forms and return them to me when you are done."

I smiled as I stared down at the clipboard with so many different papers attached to it. As I sat down and began to fill everything out, I left so many things blank. I didn't know a lot of things financially, and I knew that if Jason were here, I could ask him. I got up and walked back to the receptionist to return the clipboard.

The receptionist smiled at me as I handed it back. As I began to turn to sit down, she said, "Miss, I'm going to need proof of ID and insurance card."

I turned, got close to her, and said, "Um, I don't have my insurance card. It's through my husband's work."

She looked at me and said, "Okay, I can make a phone call. The nurse will call you back once I have all your paperwork ready."

I didn't know who she was going to call, but I figured I was in the clear. I sat down and was staring at the woman across from me, who was also by herself.

She looked up at me as she held a magazine and said, "Are you nervous?"

I laughed and said, "A little."

"Are you pregnant?" she asked.

I nodded and said, "How far are you?"

"Seven months."

"Wow, you are so tiny," I said.

She laughed and said, "Everyone shows differently, I guess. I feel so big though! How far are you?"

"Oh, well I'm not sure," I said.

She looked at me, and before she was able to say anything, I heard my name being called.

"Laurie Benk."

"Good luck!" she said as I got up and walked over to the nurse.

"Hi," I said as I greeted the nurse wearing pink scrubs.

"Hello, follow me, please."

I followed her into a long hall and sat down in a chair as she took my vitals. She told me to get on the scale, and it read 143 pounds. I was shocked.

The nurse could tell something was wrong as my eyes widened. She said, "Are you okay?"

"I gained weight."

She removed a pen from her pocket and began to take notes. She got on her computer and said, "I'm going to ask a few questions if that's okay?"

"Yes," I said nervously.

"Great, when was your last Pap?"

"Oh, I don't know... It's been a while," I said.

"What is a while? Over one year?"

I nodded.

"Okay, when was your last menstrual cycle?"

"Well, from what I can remember, it was...I think... March... I don't know the exact date..."

"Okay, have you been sexually active?"

I laughed and said, "Yes, with my husband."

"Any history of anxiety, depression, or suicidal thoughts?"

I shook my head. I knew it was bad to lie, but I didn't want to dive into anything with a nurse I didn't know.

"Are you on any medications?"

I shook my head again.

She stood up, and I followed her into a room where a paper gown was folded neatly on the exam table.

"You'll need to undress, and the opening will be to the front. The doctor will be with you soon."

As she shut the door, I started to feel a wave of emotions. I began to undress and put the paper gown on. I looked down at my unshaven legs, my unpainted toenails, and began to get the shivers. I felt more nude than what I really was. I felt exposed. I was waiting for a doctor to talk to me about a pregnancy that not even my own husband was aware of. I began picking at the paper that was on the bed.

Just then, I heard a knock on the door, and I saw an older man with white hair, white beard, and blue eyes walk inside with a nurse.

"Hello, Mrs. Benk, my name is Dr. Burtley. How are you today?"

"Hello. I'm nervous," I said.

"That's normal. Let's see how this pregnancy is going, shall we?" he said as he smiled and washed his hands in the small sink that was in the room. "Okay, let's have you lie down, and I'm going to do an exam first, and then we will go from there."

I lay down on the small green exam table, the paper robe and paper gown crinkling as I lay flat. I was staring up at the light and trying to relax myself as the doctor began to check my stomach.

"What was the date of your last menstrual cycle?" he asked.

"I told the nurse… It was sometime in March."

"Oh?" he said. "That would make you around six months or so. But we will check to confirm."

As I sat up and tried to cover myself, some of the paper robe tore here and there. I felt silly wearing it.

Just then, the nurse said, "Oh, don't worry about the tear. We didn't get your urine sample. Would you mind dressing and leaving one to confirm the positive pregnancy?"

I nodded, and before the doctor left, he handed me a small plastic bag filled with pamphlets for first-time parents, a sample of prenatal vitamins, and a small card from the office that said, "Welcome to our office!" I smiled at the doctor and nurse as they left the room.

I got dressed quickly and opened the door to walk across the hall to the bathroom. There was a small specimen cup with my name on it. Just as I finished the urine test, I began washing my hands and was staring at myself in the mirror. I raised my hoodie, turned to the side, and looked at my belly. I grabbed my phone and took a picture, the first and only picture I had taken of myself since I found out I was pregnant. I walked out of the bathroom and went back to the room as I waited for the doctor and nurse to come back.

I got a phone call. I didn't recognize the number, but whoever it was kept calling, so I decided to answer. "Hello?"

"Hello, this is Cliff calling for Laurie Benk?"

"This is Laurie," I said.

"Great. Well, I just arrived at your home, but no one is answering. I'm sorry, but we are gonna have to reschedule the delivery. The next one available is in about a month."

I was so confused and asked, "Wait, what delivery?"

"The baby furniture?" he said.

"Oh, it arrived? I wasn't told," I said angrily.

"I apologize, but that's not my department. I'm just here to deliver…" he said, sounding frustrated.

"Well, I need that furniture. Can you wait for me to get home? I am at an appointment."

I heard him sigh as he said, "I can't do that. I have other deliveries."

"Please. Look, I need that furniture, and I can't do it by myself."

He sighed again and said, "Uh…okay, I guess that's fine."

"Thank you! I will try to hurry," I said as I hung up.

Time passed, and I was still sitting in the room, staring at the clock on the wall. I started to bite my nails as I waited, but no one was coming inside the room. I stood up, took a peek into the hall, saw the nurse who had been in the room with me and the doctor earlier, and said, "Um, excuse me, something came up, and I need to go."

The nurse looked at me, came closer, and said, "Ma'am, you need to stay; we haven't finished your appointment."

"You don't understand; I need to head home." I brushed past the nurse.

She continued to call, "Mrs. Benk!" as I was hurrying away.

I ignored her and left. I walked out of the office so fast I felt as if they were chasing me, but when I looked back, no one was there. I got in my car and drove out of the parking lot. I grabbed my phone, put in my address, and began rushing home.

I was speeding, and my phone began ringing. It was the doctor's office. I didn't answer. They left a voice mail, but I didn't bother to check it.

"I'll listen to you when I get home," I said as I silenced my phone.

I ran a few red lights and stop signs. I kept thinking I was going to get pulled over, but thankfully I didn't. Instead, I got a lot of honks, and a few people gave me the finger.

My phone rang again, and it was Cliff. "Hello?"

"Hi, I'm running late for deliveries. I'm going to head out."

"No, no, no! Please. I'm almost there. I ran out of my doctor's appointment!" I said.

"Ugh, okay," he said as I hit End.

I needed to hurry.

As I pulled in front of my house, I saw the large truck. Cliff was sitting in the front seat, and another man was in the passenger seat. Cliff saw me and grinned with relief that I'd finally arrived.

"Hi, I'm sorry...I was...at my doctor's appointment... but let me...open the door," I said as I was trying to catch my breath.

"Ma'am, are you okay?" he said as he got closer to me.

"I'm fine. I was just rushing," I said.

"Well, don't hurt yourself," he said with a giggle.

I walked over to the garage keypad and opened the garage. We walked inside, and Cliff said, "So, where would you like everything?"

I led him upstairs and turned on the light to the nursery.

Cliff looked around the room and at the walls. He turned to me and said, "Did you paint the room?"

I smiled and said, "Yeah, all by myself."

He looked at me. "Nice. Sorry, I'll get started," he said as he went downstairs and headed out to the truck.

I sat down in the hallway and tried to catch my breath. I looked down at the phone in my hand and saw that I had a missed call from Perla also.

I watched as the two men came up the stairs and started to assemble a beautiful grey baby crib, a matching grey dresser, and a white rocking chair.

I stood up and walked over to the new furniture. I slid my hand across the dresser. I smiled as I envisioned small onesies placed in the drawers. I walked over to the crib and pushed down in the center of the crib, making sure it was secure. I finally sat down on the rocking chair and began to rock myself.

The men stood in the room and said, "We're done. Thank you!"

I didn't bother to get up. I looked at them and said, "Thanks, I'll lock up right now."

They headed downstairs and shut the door.

I shut my eyes and placed my hands on my belly as I rocked back and forth. I felt small kicks. I laughed and said, "This is your room." It was so quiet in the house that

I could only hear the gentle glide of the chair. I placed my head back on the chair and dozed off. I was so tired from the day. I felt more complete knowing everything was finally here.

* * * * *

I awoke to my phone ringing. I sat up and walked over to the dresser, where I'd placed it, and saw that Perla was calling me again. I answered and said, "Hello?"

"Hi, Laurie! I wanted to call you to see how your appointment went?"

"Oh, my appointment?" I said.

"Yeah! It was today, right?" she asked.

"Yeah, yeah, it was. It was great!"

"What'd the doctor say? How far along are you?"

I didn't want to tell her that I'd walked out in the middle of my appointment. So, I lied and said, "He did an exam and gave me a bag of my prenatals."

"So, how far along are you?"

I hesitated before I said, "He said almost six months."

"Wow, you are farther along than I thought!" she exclaimed.

"Yeah, I didn't realize. But it makes sense with how off I was feeling," I said.

"Well, you would be surprised how common it is to not know how far you are, especially with all the stress you've been under."

Just as I was about to say something, I heard what sounded like the front door opening. I stepped slowly into the hallway and started to walk towards the staircase.

"Laurie?" Perla said.

"Um, Can I call you right back?" I said.

"Yeah, sure."

I hung up the phone and held it close to my chest. The house was dark. I'd fallen asleep, so all the lights were off.

I forgot to lock the door! I thought to myself.

I started walking slowly downstairs and felt a slight breeze come inside the house. My heart was pounding as I inched down step-by-step.

I'd reached the middle of the stairs when suddenly I heard a voice call out, "Laurie!" It was Jason.

I ran downstairs and flipped the switch on quickly. The door was still open, and I shut and locked it. I turned around to see where he was, but I couldn't see him. I walked into the kitchen, turned on the light, and said, "Jason, you scared me."

But there was no one.

I just stood there. I knew I'd heard him. The door was open, and I clearly heard him call out for me. I began to shake at the thought that Jason wasn't really there. I saw the pills on the counter and walked over to them. I grabbed the bottle with my hands that were still shaking, opened it, took a pill, and poured myself water from the kitchen sink. I drank it quickly.

As I finished the water, I started to walk around the house. I opened the pantry, garage, and closets. I looked in small crevices and even under the bed, but I didn't find anything. I must have been so stressed that I hoped to see Jason, especially for the appointment today. But he wasn't here.

I left the lights on and double-checked the locks. I checked my phone, and there was nothing. I started to go upstairs, and I kept looking behind me. I felt uneasy.

"I need to go to bed," I said out loud to myself.

I walked to the bathroom and washed my face. I shut my eyes as I rubbed the soap on my cheeks. After I rinsed off, I opened my eyes and stared at myself in the mirror. I looked so tired. I felt as though the more tired I was, the more my face was slowly starting to change. I was noticing lines that were not there just a few weeks ago. I noticed the dark spots under my eyes looked darker, and my lips looked cracked.

I stepped back and looked up at the bathroom light. "It has to be the lighting," I said as I turned off the light and went to bed.

I sat up in bed, grabbed my phone, and called Perla back. "Hey, sorry, are you busy?"

"Hey, Laurie, are you okay?"

"Yeah, I'm just missing Jason," I said.

"Is it because of the appointment today?" she asked.

"Yeah, I think I'm realizing that I'm going to do this alone," I said as tears started to fall down my cheeks.

"Aw, Laurie. I'm sorry you're crying. Do you need me to stop by?"

"No, it's okay. I'm just starting to process it all," I said.

"Well, you're not alone; you can call me anytime," she said.

"Thank you, I better get some sleep. I'm definitely feeling pretty tired."

"Oh, by the way. Did you talk to Dr. Burtley about the symptoms you mentioned to me?" she asked.

I could feel my eyelids weighing down. I lied and said, "Oh, he said it was all normal."

"Oh. Well, okay. I'll let you get some sleep then. Good night!"

"Night!" I said as I hung up.

I put my phone on the nightstand and dozed off. I could feel my body weigh down into my bed. My bedsheets started to feel stuck to me. I felt as though I was getting hot all of a sudden. I knew I was asleep, or I thought I was asleep. But I could hear everything around me. I opened my eyes, but couldn't move my body. I lay still. I tried to make my finger flinch. I was staring at my hand, but nothing was moving. I had no idea what was going on.

I heard a noise in the hallway. I was hoping that it was Jason coming home and that he would walk inside the room and help me with whatever was going on. But I was too scared to see what the noise was. It was getting louder and louder. It sounded like someone running down the hall and suddenly stopping at my doorway. I heard the creaking sound of the door. I was staring at the door, waiting.

I knew my eyes were wide open, but I felt as if I was barely awake. I felt a sudden shooting pain in my lower belly. I shut my eyes and drifted away, further into my body. I wanted to wake up, but I had no control over what was happening.

Chapter 14

I was scared to go to sleep at night. I often fell asleep throughout the day on the couch, but less and less in my own room.

I needed to try to finish the last of the nursery. I grabbed the onesies and blankets that I had set aside and started to place them in the drawers. I placed a teddy bear on the dresser, and several empty picture frames on it as well. I couldn't wait until there were actual photos in the frames.

I started to work on the mobile for the baby crib. As soon as I placed the battery inside, I turned on the mobile and listened to the slow lullaby that it played. I attached it to the crib and turned it on as I finished putting the blankets away; the music was soothing.

I walked around the nursery and was so happy it was complete. It wasn't a gym or an office, but in the end, it was what I wanted it to be—a nursery.

I heard my phone, and when I grabbed it from the side pocket of my sweat pants, I saw it was Jason. I was nervous about picking it up. I calmly answered and said, "Hello?"

"Hey, Laurie," Jason said sternly.

"Are you coming home?" I asked.

"No, I have a question," he said.

"Yeah?"

"I got a voice mail from a doctor's office saying they wanted to verify my insurance. I haven't called them back, but I just wanted to ask if you'd gone to a doctor?"

"No, I haven't seen any doctor," I said.

"Okay. Well, it has to be a mistake then. I was just calling to check."

"Okay. Well, I need to eat. I'm so hungry," I said.

"Sorry, did I interrupt you during your class? It's not even your lunch break, right?"

I never told Jason about work. He knew I took a few days off when I wasn't doing well, but I never told him that I wasn't working anymore.

"Oh, we're in the switch-off. Perla has my class right now," I lied.

"Well, I'll stay in touch. Talk to you later," he said.

I walked over to the crib, turned on the mobile, and reached for the teddy bear that I had placed on the dresser. I sat down in the rocking chair and watched as the mobile spun in a slow clockwise motion. I stared at the small little animals, which hung from the mobile; they were swinging and swaying. I was in a daze as I heard the lullaby play. I could feel the chair rock back and forth.

I held the teddy bear as if it were my baby. I smiled and stared at the black buttons for eyes and the furry brown coat and said, "This is gonna be the baby's room, and you

are gonna take good care of the baby when it's nighttime."
I stared at the bear as I rocked back and forth. I shut my
eyes, listening to the music from the mobile.

* * * * *

I was still in the chair as my eyes began to slowly open; the
room was dark now. The streetlight was shining through
the window. I was fixated on the mobile; the lullaby was
not playing. The animals that hung from the mobile were
still swaying, as if a light breeze had passed by and caused
them to move.

I sat there, unable to move. I couldn't believe this was
happening again. I couldn't move. I was awake, but my
body was frozen, stuck to the rocking chair. I looked down
and saw my hands were empty; they lay loose on my lap.
I could feel my eyes shift, looking for the teddy bear. I saw
it lying on the floor.

I began to panic. I felt my eyes water, knowing that
I had dropped the bear that I fell asleep with. *What if that
was my baby?* I thought. *I fell asleep for what seemed like a few
moments and dropped it. I'm going to be a horrible mother.*

I could feel my breathing quicken. I was trying to
connect to my body, to wake up. I couldn't close my eyes;
I was still frozen. I wanted to scream, I wanted to yell, but
I was trapped inside myself. *What if that was my baby, and
I couldn't get up?* I was trying to focus on anything that
would get me to stand up, but nothing was working.

As I sat frozen in the chair, I began to feel it sway
forward and slowly fall back. I wasn't moving, so what

was moving me? With each sway, I leaned farther back and then farther forward. I couldn't grip to hold on.

I felt my body shift and fall hard on the floor. I lay there still frozen. I couldn't move my head, only my eyes. I could hear the rocking chair continue to go back and forth, but I couldn't see what was causing it to move. I stared at the teddy bear that was lying on the floor next to me.

Slowly, I felt my hands loosen up, then my legs unwind, and my neck lose stiffness. I began to blink quickly, and the only thing I could do was scream. I couldn't stop screaming.

* * * * *

I opened my eyes. I didn't remember going to sleep again. I just remembered yelling and yelling, but I must have exhausted myself until I slept. I tried sitting up and felt extremely dizzy. I had no idea what time it was. The sun was blaring through the window. I stared at the small rug on the floor and saw several small drops of blood. I touched my forehead, and it felt bruised.

My baby! I thought. *I don't know how hard I fell. How long have I been bleeding?*

I tried to stand up, but it felt as though the room were fading in and out. I had no energy. I felt faint and dizzy. I looked around the room as I lay on the floor, leaning on my arms. I saw my phone still sitting on the dresser. I wasn't sure if I could reach it, but I had to try. I was sliding on the floor like a worm; any energy I tried to use to get up was immediately spent. I couldn't put weight on my body. I was just too tired and too dizzy.

As I slid across the floor, I turned and touched the dresser. I held the handle of a drawer to try to pull myself up. I leaned against the dresser and caught my breath. I could hear my heart pounding in my ears. I shut my eyes for a moment, caught my breath, and held my belly. I looked up and saw my phone towards the edge of the dresser. I held the drawer handle and tried to shake the dresser to get the phone to fall.

"C'mon, Laurie," I said out loud.

I held the handle and tried to reach up. I could feel my weak arms tire as I raised them up once more; then the tip of my fingers touched my phone, and I saw it slam to the floor. I exhaled with relief as I grabbed it.

I wasn't sure whom to call, but I knew I had to call someone. My head felt fuzzy, as if the sparks in my brain were slowly losing connectivity. I felt myself drift in and out of wanting to shut my eyes. I held my phone, quickly scrolled through the list, and started to call someone in my recent contacts.

I could feel my vision begin to blur, and suddenly I heard a man's voice. I had called Jason, and he'd answered.

"Hello…please don't hang up… I fell. I'm bleeding… and I can't…move."

I heard Jason screaming my name over the phone. He sounded so distant, as if I were falling down a well, deeper and deeper, as if Jason was completely out of reach.

* * * * *

I woke up in a panic. I loudly exhaled and lay still because it seemed my body was badly bruised. I felt a blanket on me, and I was lying on an uncomfortable pillow. I opened my eyes. I was in a room with a small chair. I began to look around. I had an IV in my arm. I stared at the fluid that was dripping slowly into my vein. I tried to lift my arm, but saw that both of them were tied to the sides of this strange hospital bed.

"Someone help me!" I shouted as I shook my wrists. I could feel the tightness of the band rubbing against my wrist.

Just then, a nurse ran in and said, "Okay, you need to try to relax. Okay?"

"Why am I tied down? Why!" I yelled.

"Ma'am, please, the doctor will be in shortly." She was searching her pocket and pulled out a small orange vile. She started to attach it to my IV.

"No, no, what is it? You don't understand…my baby! My baby!" I shouted.

"You just need to calm down, ma'am," she said as she continued to attach the vile.

I stared at her as I suddenly felt the room spin. I knew I was going to drift off into a deep sleep, but I was fighting to stay awake.

* * * * *

"Laurie," a familiar voice said.

I started to slowly wake up. I knew it was Jason. He was finally here with me. I tried to move, and I realized I was still tied to the bed. I blinked several times; my eyes felt so dry. It pained me to open them. I opened my mouth, trying to speak; my voice was hoarse.

I saw Jason sitting next to me. He was dressed in a black suit, he had the top button of his shirt undone, and I could smell his strong, musky cologne.

"J-Jas-son…wh-where am I-I?" I stammered.

He exhaled and said, "Laurie, you're safe."

"No, where am I?" I said again.

He looked down at me and said, "You are in the hospital. You had an accident. You've been asleep for over thirty hours now."

I was in shock; my body felt numb. "Why am I tied to the bed?"

Jason glanced down at the restraints and back up at me. He looked angry. There was no empathy, no sense of urgency to try to help me.

"Laurie, I told you, you needed help. You didn't listen to me," he said.

I was confused.

He stood up and walked over to a small table by the door. It looked as if there was a file there with a phone on top of it, my phone. He grabbed it, looked as if he was searching for something on my phone, then suddenly stood still, and said, "You aren't working at the school anymore?"

I shook my head.

"You never told me," he said.

I stared at him, looking him in the eyes, and asked, "Have you been home?" My voice was low.

"Yes." He walked over to me. "You know, I wondered what you spent so much money on, what you ordered.

To be honest, I thought it was a new wardrobe; then I thought…you were leaving me," he said quietly.

"No, Jason. I thought, being home, I could work on the baby's room, and I—"

Jason yelled, "Laurie…stop!"

I got goose bumps; this wasn't the reaction I was expecting.

"Jason…please, our baby…is our baby…okay?" I said as tears started to fall from my eyes. I was trying to wiggle my arms.

Jason walked over to me and said, "Laurie, please!"

I could feel myself begin to panic. I suddenly felt as if the world were caving in on me. "Jason, what is going on?"

Jason looked at me sternly. He came to me and said, "Laurie, do you not remember anything?"

"Jason, I was in the rocking chair, and I was pushed off somehow…I slid or…" I stopped as I tried to remember, but as I was explaining myself, I realized what I was saying made no sense.

"Laurie, you did this to yourself. That is why you are in restraints."

"No, why would I hurt myself…my baby," I said.

Jason got my phone and placed it in a clear bag. He grabbed the file that was on the table and said, "When you're ready, I will talk about what needs to happen next. Right now, you need to rest. You really did a number on yourself this time, Laurie."

As he left the room, a nurse came in and said, "Hi, I'm going to be helping you during your recovery. I'm going to be in and out. I have to administer your medication and change some bandages."

I looked at her, confused. "What bandages?"

She looked at me and said nothing. It was as if I'd never spoken. I felt invisible. I watched her as she administered the same small orange vile that the other nurse had given me just before I fell asleep.

"No, I don't want to sleep," I said.

She said nothing. As the fluid made its way into my system, she stood next to me and put on blue latex gloves. She stood there and stared at me, waiting for me to drift off to a deep sleep.

* * * * *

There were visions of different nurses. I remember my eyes opening and closing every now and then. I would see what looked like blue gloves tinged with blood, dirty bandages, and blanket after blanket. Every now and then, I would feel a cool sensation on my right arm, where the IV was. When I felt that, I knew I would fall asleep.

There was no sense of time. I had no idea what was going on around me. I knew I was still in restraints. Occasionally, I felt aches and pains. I would exhale as I felt small stabbing sensations throughout my belly, my head would pound, and the only thing that made it better was when I slept.

But I didn't want to sleep anymore. I needed to wake up.

Chapter 15

I was in and out of sleep for what must have been weeks. I was in a daze; whatever medication was being given to me through the IV was keeping me in a constant state of sleep. I was essentially a zombie, numb to my surroundings and to my own body. I was aware of where I was and what was going on around me, but physically I felt nothing.

One day, Jason came in the room and closed the door behind him. He sat in the chair that was next to my bed. He had that file with him and didn't even look at me when he opened it and said, "So, what happened?"

I sat there knowing he wanted some explanation for all of this, but I had none to give. "Why don't you tell me, Jason. I'm the one tied to this bed," I said sarcastically.

He scoffed as he said, "Laurie, I'm trying to help you."

"If you are trying to help me, then why am I still tied to this bed?" I asked.

He looked at me and said, "Laurie, do you remember hurting yourself? You were starving yourself. You are extremely malnourished; you've lost some weight."

"Jason...I wouldn't do that to myself...I was sick. But it was from the pregnancy."

Jason sighed as he angrily said, "Laurie, you were never pregnant!"

"What?" I said. I felt as though I had just swallowed my throat, and it had fallen to the deepest pit of my stomach.

"Laurie...stay calm."

"No, how can I stay calm after what you just said?"

"Laurie, listen, please," he said.

Shaking, I looked at him and said, "Please take off the restraints. I'm not going to do anything. I just...I need to check something. Please," I begged.

Jason looked at me and said, "I can't do that."

"Why?!" I shouted.

"Laurie, this move was supposed to help you. No one here knows us, and now...now they do."

"What do you mean?" I asked.

"Laurie, you need my help." As Jason said this, he took a paper from the file and told me that he was recommending intense treatment.

"You want to admit me to this psych hospital?"

"The hospital that I work in; you will see me all the time," he said as if it would make it better.

"But you are going to be my doctor again?" I asked.

"Yes," he said sternly.

"Not my husband?" I looked him in the eyes, waiting for his answer.

"Laurie, when you are done with treatment, you can come back home." He didn't answer my question. He began signing some papers in front of me and said, "So, since you lack the capacity to do so, I will sign these forms for you; they say that you are now under my care until further notice. I think this is best."

I didn't know what to say. I felt helpless. I didn't have the energy to fight. Just as I laid my head back, trying to convince myself to accept my fate, I couldn't stop thinking about my baby. I know Jason said I wasn't pregnant, but I didn't believe it. I couldn't believe it.

* * * * *

The time passed slowly, I had no idea how long I had been there. I had to be watched with everything I did, from going to the bathroom, to taking a shower, and even eating. There wasn't a TV in my room, nothing to help me pass the time. I was just alone in a room, with only my thoughts. I hadn't seen Jason in a while. There were just nurses coming in and out of the room. I tried to make conversation, but they wouldn't even look at me; they just handed me my pills in the morning and at night, and walked out of the room.

My body felt achy still. I knew I fell, but I didn't realize that I would feel like this for so long. I couldn't stop thinking about the fact that Jason said I hurt myself. I had no memory of that. The more I closed my eyes trying to think of what happened, the more the same memories replayed in my head.

"Think, Laurie," I said out loud in bed.

Just then, there was a knock on the door. I sat up in bed and watched as a nurse walked in.

"Hello, Laurie, would you like to come out and eat in the hall before you take your medicine?"

"No, I want to go home."

The nurse looked at her chart and said, "Dr. Benk said it would be good for you to socialize."

I laughed and said, "My husband thinks so?"

I knew she knew I was being sarcastic. She didn't say anything, just looked at me. I didn't feel like being around people, but I was tired of that room. I stood up, and the nurse came over to me and said, "Take it easy, Laurie."

I looked at her as she tried to help me. I pulled my arm away from her. I wanted to prove that I didn't want anyone to help me.

I walked out and saw a few people sitting at small round tables. The entire cafeteria smelled like Clorox. It was almost too clean to sit and eat. I sat down at a table next to a woman who had grey hair.

She sat quietly and ate her apple. After I was seated, she looked at me and said, "You are new."

I laughed. "How long have you been here?" I asked.

"Long enough," she said.

She didn't look crazy. I wondered why she was even there. I stared at her long grey hair; small pieces of black hair poked through. I smiled at the thought that she'd been young once and not in this place. She had moles on her face and long eyelashes, but very small eyes.

She caught me staring at her and said, "Are you okay?"

"I'm sorry; it's been so long since I've talked to someone. I don't even know how long I've been here."

"It's all those pills," she said.

I looked at her and said, "You take them too?"

"They think I do," she said with a grin.

I sat with her at the table and looked over at the nurses as they started to come around with the tray of pills for the patients that were eating in the hall. It was almost time to go back to our rooms. A nurse came by with a small tray holding little jars of pills with the last names of the patients on them.

She walked over to our table, holding the jar that had "Dillon" on it. She looked at the woman next to me and said, "Ready, Ms. Dillon?"

The grey-haired woman smiled and opened her mouth as the nurse poured the pills inside. I saw her swallow and then open her mouth.

"Clear," the nurse said. She turned to me. "Ready, Mrs. Benk?"

I nodded, and she poured the pills in my mouth. I swallowed them, and I opened my mouth.

She said, "Clear," and walked to the next table.

Ms. Dillon looked around to make sure no one was watching. Then, she looked at me and lifted her tongue. The two pills were sitting there.

I looked at her in amazement. I could have sworn I saw her swallow the pills. "How long have you not been taking your pills?" I asked.

"Long enough," she said.

I saw her pick up the apple and shove the pills inside a hollowed-out area she'd carved with her teeth. She put the apple on her food tray, got up, and threw it away. She came back to sit next to me and said, "Benk? As in Dr. Benk?"

I nodded my head. "I'm his wife," I said.

Her eyes widened and she said, "You're married to the doctor of this place?"

"Yeah."

"Why?" she said.

"I fell in love," I said with a laugh.

She looked at me and said, "Well, if you're married, where's your ring?"

I looked down at my hand and said, "He must be holding on to it."

The nurse called out, "Okay, time to head back."

Everyone got up and threw their food away. As we walked back to our rooms, some people were dragging their feet. I could feel myself getting tired. The only one who didn't seem to be sleepy at all was Ms. Dillon.

As I walked in the room, a nurse followed me to my bed. I lay down in bed, and she covered me with a blanket.

"Get some rest," she said.

It was still light out. I suppose I would sleep away my days here.

Chapter 16

It had been five years. There was no clock, no calendar, no sense of time. I only knew because I heard the nurses wish each other "Happy New Year" five times. I couldn't believe how long I had been here.

The routine hadn't changed. I woke up in the morning, bathed with a nurse watching me and helping me dress before eating breakfast in my room. For lunch, I could eat in the main hall with the other patients, where we were given our morning pills. I came back to the room, slept until dinner, ate, and slept again. No one here knew anyone. No one spoke to anyone. We might eat in the same room at times, but with the little time we were given to eat, we focused on our food and not on communicating.

I hadn't seen Jason in five years. He never came by to visit me. I just saw the same nurses. I would often ask about him, but after a while, I remembered that he said he couldn't be my husband and my doctor at the same time. At times, I wondered if he still loved me. I felt comforted when the nurses still addressed me as Mrs. Benk. That was a good sign. I was still married.

I missed talking to Perla. I thought about her and wondered what she thought about me being here.

* * * * *

"Mrs. Benk, would you like to have lunch in the hall today?"

I nodded and walked with the nurse out into the hall. I walked over to Ms. Dillon and sat next to her. She was carving out her apple with her teeth. She smiled at me, and I noticed she had an extra apple on her tray.

I began to eat, and she put the apple on my tray. I looked at her and said, "I don't feel like an apple."

"You don't need to eat it," she said.

I put it back on her tray, and she quickly grabbed it, placed it back on my tray, and said, "Mrs. Benk, do as I do." She looked at the nurses who were preparing to hand out the pills.

I grabbed the apple and quickly began to carve out the apple with my teeth, as she did.

The nurse came by and said, "Ms. Dillon, ready for your pills?"

I saw as she placed the pills in her mouth. And what looked like her swallowing the pills was actually her using her tongue to tuck the pills away.

She opened her mouth, and the nurse said, "Clear."

The nurse turned to me and said, "Mrs. Benk, are you ready for your pills?"

I opened my mouth and did the same. I felt the pills underneath my tongue slowly start to disintegrate with my saliva. The taste was horrible.

"Clear," the nurse said after inspecting my open mouth.

I grabbed the apple and pretended to take a bite. Instead, with my tongue, I quickly placed the pills inside the apple, put the apple on the tray, got up, and threw my tray away.

Ms. Dillon looked at me and said, "Stay awake."

I didn't understand what she meant.

The nurse called out, "Time to head back to your rooms."

I stared back at Ms. Dillon as I walked towards the nurse who accompanied me back to my room. She walked me to my bed, covered me, and said, "Get some rest."

I shut my eyes, but the moment I heard the door close, I opened them. I lay there awake. It was strange being up at this hour; the sun was out, but by this time, I would usually be asleep. I heard the nurses walking in the hallway.

I heard the door open and closed my eyes. Someone walked inside. I could smell the scent of Clorox being sprayed in the room. *It must be the person who comes to clean as I sleep.* I'd always wondered when they cleaned the rooms. I suppose being asleep was the best time to do so. I couldn't believe it had never awakened me.

I opened my eyes as I heard her open the bathroom door. I saw a woman inside the bathroom, cleaning up, her back facing me. She had no idea I was awake, watching her. I saw her cleaning cart, and on the top was a set of keys. I had no idea what they all led to, but I saw that underneath that set was a bright-red D-ring set of keys separate from the other ones. Attached was a car-key fob.

Don't even think about it, I thought to myself as I stared at the keys. I sat upright, trying to be as quiet as possible. I had no idea how long I would be here. It had already been too long, and I needed answers. I needed to know what really happened five years ago.

I stood up and walked over to the bathroom door. The lady didn't hear me; she was busy sweeping. I grabbed the other broom from the cart and quickly shut the door, placing the broom through the handle so she couldn't open the door. I could hear her banging on the door. I doubt it was loud enough for anyone to hear. I knew I had at least a few hours to make my next move.

I went to the cart and at the bottom saw her pink sweater. I put it on. I grabbed a rubber band, which was holding a few pens in place, and put my hair up.

I walked over to my door and slowly opened it. I could hear the nurses down the hall at the nurses' station. No one else was in the halls. I assumed everyone was asleep. I pushed the cart slowly out of my room. I closed my door and grabbed the keys. I was jumbling the keys when, written on them, I saw the numbers of the rooms. I quickly searched for my room number, grabbed my key, and locked the door. Once my door was shut, I couldn't hear the cleaning lady banging on the bathroom door. I smiled; my sudden getaway plan was starting to work.

I grabbed the cart and began walking in the opposite direction from where the nurses were. They were too preoccupied to even look up. I turned down the hall and could hear the rust from the metal wheels slowly turning. I kept my head down and barely looked up, trying to figure out where I was going. I saw an Exit sign with the arrow pointing to the stairs at the opposite end of the hall. I made my way slowly down the hall, still pushing the cart.

I was almost at the end of the hall when, just then, I passed by an office that said, "Dr. Jason Benk." I stopped. My heart began to pound. I wondered if he was in there. I could hear someone talking inside. I walked over to the door and saw Jason on the phone, sitting at his desk. He was looking out the window. He looked as if he was having an intense conversation. He had facial hair, and he was wearing a casual polo shirt. It was strange to see him looking more relaxed. I was so used to seeing him completely shaven and in suits.

As I watched him on the phone, I saw that on his desk there were two frames. I couldn't see the photos, but I recognized the frames. They were from the box of photos that had our wedding pictures in them. I had hoped that he still had us on his desk. I saw his hand on the phone and didn't see his wedding band. I was quiet as I pressed up closer to the door, trying to hear his voice.

I heard him say, "You'll see her when it's time."

I suddenly realized that he was probably married to or dating someone else. I felt as if I were losing my breath. I stopped for a moment.

"Laurie, focus," I said out loud.

I took a few steps back and continued down the hall, still pushing the cart. I reached the staircase and grabbed the keys. I opened the door and rushed down the stairs.

I had no idea where the exit was. I knew I couldn't look back. I had to keep moving forward until I got out of there.

I kept running until I saw a sign that said, "Ground Level." I walked into an underground parking lot. I grabbed the keys in my hand and pushed the alarm button on the fob. Just then, I saw a small white Honda Civic's lights go on and off. I rushed over to the car and got inside. As I did, I exhaled a sigh of relief. It had been so long since I was behind the wheel.

I started the car, and right then I realized the only place I could go—back home. Even if I wasn't going to like what I was about to see, I had to find out for myself if Jason had replaced me. If I still had a home to come to at the end of all of this, as Jason said I would.

I exited out of the parking lot, and the sun was still high in the sky. Everything looked the same. I drove the short distance home. I was getting nervous as I pulled up to the house.

I parked the car on the side of the house. There was a red Subaru parked in the driveway. I had no idea what I was going to do. I thought about ringing the doorbell, but what if no one answered? I thought about going to the back, but I didn't want to scare anyone.

I stayed calm, and suddenly my eyes were fixated on the garage keypad. I got out of the car, walked over to it, and punched in the code. "One-two-one-five-two-three," I said out loud. "Please work."

I heard the garage open.

It worked!

I was surprised. I hoped that was a good sign. It was our wedding date, after all.

Maybe he forgot to change it? I thought.

I opened the door to the house and could smell the familiar scent of our home. I shut the door behind me, and I began walking through the house and into our old living room. I froze. The walls were covered in photos, photos mostly of me. They were from the wedding. I stood there, completely motionless. My jaw was wide open. I stared at myself in my white wedding dress.

I was confused and felt as if I were in a dream. "This is still my home," I said out loud.

Just then, I heard someone in the kitchen. I turned and was met with small eyes that looked just like mine.

I bent down, and all I could say was, "Hello there, blue eyes."

I was looking at this small child, and suddenly she said, "Hi, Mommy."

CPSIA information can be obtained
at www.ICGtesting.com
Printed in the USA
BVHW091308230621
610214BV00011B/2122